R#
(23)
12

34450
B10

MERMAID
ON
WHEELS

MERMAID ON WHEELS

The Story of Margaret Lester

BY JUNE EPSTEIN

with a foreword by
D. J. E. CHESHIRE, M.B.B.S., D.Phys.Med.,
Director, Spinal Injuries Centre,
Austin Hospital, Heidelberg, Victoria.

TAPLINGER PUBLISHING COMPANY
NEW YORK

First Published in the United States in 1969 by
Taplinger Publishing Co., Inc.
New York, N.Y. 10003
Copyright © 1967 by June Epstein in Australia.

Library of Congress Catalog Card Number 67-25739
Standard Book Number 8008-5190-0
Printed in the United States of America

Second Printing

Author's Note
Mermaid on Wheels is a true story without an end. Since
I was long ago 'adopted' into Margaret's family, it is
told at first hand. Every incident is authentic, and many
of the conversations are reproduced verbatim, in some
cases because I was there when it happened.

*All royalties from sales of this book
are being donated by the author to the
Philip Ross Guest Memorial Fund
for Paraplegic Children.*

*This book has been written for Gerta and for little Phil.
It is dedicated to all who are disabled in body, but
not necessarily in spirit.*

ACKNOWLEDGMENTS

In writing this book I have been fortunate to have had the enthusiastic support and advice of Dr David Cheshire, Director of the Spinal Injuries Centre of the Austin Hospital, Heidelberg, Victoria. He has given me full access to the Centre, has checked the manuscript for accuracy, and has written the Foreword and the essay 'What is Paraplegia?' contained in the Appendix. I would like to express my thanks to him, his staff, and the many patients, ex-patients, relatives and friends who have so willingly given assistance in our joint aim to present a story of encouragement for disabled people.

My special thanks are also due to

Margaret and John Lester, John Watkins, and their relatives and friends, for information, documents and photographs

Professor Timothy Nugent, Director of the Rehabilitation-Education Center, University of Illinois, for permission to quote from *Design of Buildings to Permit their Use by the Physically Handicapped*

Leon Chatelain jnr, Past President, American Institute of Architects, Washington, D.C., for permission to quote from *Architectural Barriers—A Blueprint for Action*

The President's Committee on Employment of the Handicapped, U.S.A., for permission to quote from the above, and also from *Architectural Barriers and the Handicapped*

The National Society for Crippled Children and Adults, U.S.A., for permission to quote from the story 'Architectural Barriers' in the *Easter Seal Bulletin*

The Standards Association of Australia for permission to quote from the Preface to *Draft Australian Standard Code of Recommended Practice for Building Design Requirements for the Disabled*

Selwyn Goldsmith, Architect to the City of Norwich, for permission to quote from *Designing for the Disabled*

H. Jonas & Co. (Books) Ltd, London, for permission to quote the poem 'Even the Severed Branch' from *Springs of Indian Wisdom*

David John for taking the photographs reconstructing Margaret Lester's rehabilitation, and for other photographs used in the book; and Fred Cropley for assistance with photographic material

The *Age*, *Herald-Sun Pictorial*, and *New Idea*, all of Melbourne, the *Advertiser*, Adelaide, W. & G. Record Processing Co. Pty Ltd, Melbourne, and *Farrago*, Students' Representative Council, University of Melbourne, for permission to reproduce photographs

Dr George Bedbrook, Head of the Department of Paraplegia, Royal Perth Hospital, and the staff of the Paraplegic Unit at Shenton Park Rehabilitation Hospital, Perth, Western Australia; the Paraplegic Association of Victoria; Good Samaritan Industries, W.A.; the staff and Old Collegians of the Presbyterian

Ladies' College, Melbourne; Camberwell Grammar Old Boys' Association; Lady Paton; Sister Helen Gillies; and Ronald A. Hewson; for general assistance

Ruth Alexander, for setting the fuse

And last, but not least, Lorne Fyfe, for typing the manuscript; and Julius and Katharine-Ann, without whose loving forbearance and encouragement the work could not have been undertaken.

June Epstein
Melbourne, 30th July 1966

FOREWORD

Many books have been written about the conquest of physical disability, and a number of them are specifically concerned with paraplegia. However, most of these books have a common defect: they were written by 'outsiders' and, regardless of the author's professional skill, they left at least one reader conscious of a failure to convey true understanding of the many psychological problems inherent in paraplegia.

This book is different. The author has known Margaret and her family intimately for many years, and she participated in many of the events described. Not only does this personal involvement ensure accurate reporting, but in addition, through having lived in close touch with Margaret, her husband and her family during these years the author appreciates that paraplegia affects not only the victim but the whole family. For the paraplegic to learn to become independent and psychologically adjusted to a new way of life is only part of the problem, and June Epstein is particularly successful in describing the enormous contribution that John Lester and the Watkins family made towards Margaret's rehabilitation. At the same time she makes Margaret a very real person, and portrays those qualities of the spirit which separate a person who has conquered disability from one who has succumbed to it.

Margaret and John Lester are two very fine people. I would like to thank June Epstein for writing their story and so permitting their achievements to become known to the thousands of people who will surely read this book. With reading will come understanding, and with understanding, the community will become a little wiser, and more inclined to give Margaret, and all other disabled people, that equality of opportunity which is all they ask.

D. J. E. Cheshire,
Director, Spinal Injuries Centre,
Austin Hospital, Heidelberg, Victoria.

'I believe in ability; in an entire orientation towards the handicapped that stresses not what is wrong with them but what is right with them; that emphasises not disability but ability; that faces the fact that the "can do" in a man's life exceeds the "can't do".'

Harold Russell,
Chairman, President's Committee on
Employment of the Handicapped, U.S.A.

(Harold Russell lost both arms while serving with the U.S. Navy in World War II.)

CONTENTS

continued overleaf

Contents *continued*

Illustrations

MERMAID
ON
WHEELS

PROLOGUE

As the truck laden with drainpipes rattled along the highway from Melbourne, Bruno looked out with interest at the still unfamiliar Australian landscape. The city had been left behind; rows of suburban houses were beginning to give way to more open country. At a crossroads on a hill, roads fell away to unmade streets with new houses. Ahead, blue mountains and green trees could be seen.

'East Doncaster,' said Bill, swinging the truck over a pothole into an unmade side street. 'Job's down here.'

'Cop that lot!' he exclaimed, as they drove past an attractive small house labelled 'Blue Sky'. He pointed to the garden. An outdoor swimming pool had been constructed on the level below the house, complete with machine plant room and chain-mesh fence. The water looked temptingly cool in the morning sunlight; a girl in a blue swimsuit was swimming the length of the pool with great enjoyment. She looked up and smiled at them as they drove past.

'Pretty!' suggested Bruno, cautiously trying out his English.

'Very. What a life! Some people are lucky. Fancy having nothing else to do but swim, on a Monday morning. In your own pool. . . . Here we are.'

The truck jounced to a halt beside a building site. The men stripped to the waist and unloaded the pipes.

'Now—?' asked Bruno.

'You start digging this trench, mate. Look—with the shovel—'

'Ah—dig.'

'—and I'll go back for the next load of pipes. Be about an hour. Keep digging.'

The truck roared off. As the sun climbed higher Bruno dug until the sweat ran down his face. It was his first Australian job. The shallow depression had turned into a respectable trench when he heard a woman calling. He looked up out of the trench, leaning on his shovel. She was a middle-aged woman, in a house-dress and apron. She was panting something about a girl in the pool.

'Pool?'

'Yes—in the swimming pool.'

'Ah. In the water?'

'Yes—please could you help her?'

Bruno knew the words girl, water, help, and thanked heaven he was a strong swimmer. Flinging aside his shovel, he leapt out of the trench and ran in the direction of the house, the woman puffing after him. As he approached the chain-mesh fence he saw the dark head of the girl in the blue swimsuit. She appeared to be floating face down in the water. He tugged at the gate. It was locked. Retreating a little, he vaulted the fence in one leap and ran to the water's edge.

The girl looked up at him and smiled.

Bruno halted in astonishment, almost in the act of jumping into the water. He turned bewildered to the woman who was now standing at the fence, nodding at him. 'Please would you lift her out of the water?'

'Lift?'

'She can't get out by herself. She's been in a long time.'

'Not understand.' He shook his head.

The girl tried to explain. 'I can't get out. Please help me.' She pointed to the side of the pool.

Ah! Of course. She was pointing to a wheelchair. Now Bruno understood. He had scarcely noticed it before, because one does not usually associate a wheelchair with a girl swimming in a pool. He knelt down. She put one arm around his neck, and with a great effort, for she was heavier than she looked, he stood up,

xiv

holding her carefully. Her legs dangled uselessly. He was reminded momentarily of a film he had once seen in which a man had captured a mermaid and carried her home.

'Please put me in the wheelchair. Thank you very much.'

She pulled a towel around her shoulders and wheeled herself rapidly to the locked gate. Bruno watched her bend down and extract a key from a small purse on the footplate of her chair. She unlocked the gate and held it open for him.

'Thanks for rescuing me,' she said, speaking slowly so that he would understand. 'It's the first time I've been in the pool quite by myself, and unfortunately the hoist wasn't working. The Board of Works turned the water off and I didn't see the notice!' She demonstrated with her hands the hydraulic hoist that she used to raise herself out of the water.

Bruno nodded. He walked thoughtfully back to his trench. He had seen a few disabled people back in his home country, but he had never realized that a person who could not walk might perhaps be able to swim.

When Bill returned with the second load of pipes he explained, in his halting English, what had happened.

'Was that the girl we saw in the pool on the way to work?'

'Yes. . . . Look now—the same girl!' Bruno said in surprise. A car had pulled up at their site and his mermaid was leaning out of the driving side.

'I wanted to say thank you again,' she said, smiling.

Bruno nodded in embarrassment.

She was dressed now in a bright cotton frock. The car seemed crammed to the roof. The wheelchair was folded beside her, a baby in a car-seat waved fat arms above it; two lively little girls bounced up and down on the back seat.

The men watched the girl expertly turn the car and drive away.

'I feel sorry for anyone who is crippled,' said Bill, 'but fancy that happening to the mother of three kids.'

Bruno nodded, because it was the simplest thing to do. Had his English been more adequate he would perhaps have said that he himself didn't feel sorry for the girl. It was impossible to feel pity for anyone who radiated such happiness.

As it happened, Bill was wrong on several counts. 'That' had not happened to the mother of three children; and the one thing that could rouse Bruno's mermaid to fury was to be called crippled.

xv

one || EARLY LIFE

The incinerator in the back garden at Dean Avenue, East St Kilda, in suburban Melbourne, was usually crammed full to overflowing with papers and prunings, the lid often perched on top of all at a crazy angle. The house gave somewhat the same impression, a roof crammed down on to a small container from which children, adults, wheeled toys, and dogs continually spilled out. There always seemed to be more people than actually lived there, for the Watkins family attracted friends and relatives as honey attracts bees.

The person who might reasonably be expected to object most to hearing her home compared with an overflowing incinerator was the one who would most have enjoyed the description: Gerta, the mother, who combined freedom and discipline in an admirable way. Adventurous, slightly reckless, loving, impulsive, an artist not only in pottery and metal-beating but also in all the feminine wiles, she was adored by her husband and family and friends. Nobody ever quite knew what she would do next—but one thing was certain, she and everyone around her would extract the maximum enjoyment out of every situation. The father of the family, John Watkins, an aeronautical engineer in the early stages

17

of what was to be a brilliant career, was a quieter character. But he too possessed an adventurous spirit which was constantly rekindled by Gerta's infectious gaiety. The children therefore had a double inheritance of this relish for life, and the capacity for delighted laughter at things great and small.

Margaret Anne, the eldest, had these gifts to a marked degree; she had also an inborn sense of responsibility which would be developed to the full by her rôle of eldest sister. She was a radiant, lovable little girl. People thought it a pity that such a beautiful child had to wear ugly iron and leather calipers because her legs did not seem to be growing straight. But she was taught to wear them without resentment, even though they curbed many of her childish activities. Her parents had promised her that the braces would help her to have straight, beautiful legs. She had never known them to break their word; so she waited patiently for the day when the braces would be discarded.

It was fun growing up in a rumbustious Australian family, with plenty of playmates. There was her little sister Natalie to love and fight and share things with. After Natalie came Ian, who soon had a little brother, Phillip, for his own special companion. With young, lively parents life was never dull.

There was the time John decided his children should learn to climb. He fastened a rope on the wheel-of-fire tree, and told his admiring young audience to watch while he showed them how to use it. Whereupon he fell down and split his pants. There was the party for which John and Gerta got a jeep from somewhere and everyone piled in with their best clothes and balloons, to be driven screaming with delight around the block. Even better was the 'aeroplane' John constructed by putting wooden wings on a wheelbarrow and driving a propeller from the wheel. He rushed about the garden pushing delighted children; the faster he pushed, the faster spun the propeller.

Margaret Anne's first adventure was in a basket when her young parents took her skiing and warmed her milk on a spirit lamp in the snow. She was too young to remember that occasion or subsequent ones when she travelled cheerfully in the back of their tiny car all over Victoria or interstate. But as she grew older and more children were added to the family group, vivid memories began to store up in her mind. The little car used to seem full when John and Gerta sat in the front and the baby lay in the

18

basket on the back seat. Now Margot, as she was called, was part of a noisy conglomeration of children packed in among the luggage, with petrol tins, prams, surfboard and surf ski on the roof, and bikes strapped along the front and rear bumper bars. Petrol was rationed in those latter war days, but John would bike to work for months to save his rations for a holiday trip. Once they had reached their destination, a rented cottage or a flapping canvas tent, they'd take to the bikes again. Sharing out the children, the two parents would pedal them around and show them every cliff, shoreline, tree, cave or animal within reach. During the war their holidays were spent at Phillip Island, a small picturesque island in Westernport Bay, famous for its koalas, fairy penguins and seals. When petrol rationing ended they returned to their favourite spot, Lorne, on the South coast, where they swam, rode the breakers, and fished with spears.

At home there were trees to climb, cubby-houses to build. On wet days the girls sewed and knitted dolls' clothes. Best of all, Gerta allowed them to cook as much as they liked.

Although school lessons and religious training were taken very seriously, the children knew that routines could be abandoned at a moment's notice if some exciting opportunity turned up for them that might never come again; because education was in living, not in merely thinking about it. People, too, mattered intensely. Time and again Margot saw her mother give up precious leisure to make someone else happy.

Margot started both kindergarten and music lessons almost at the same time because Miss Shand, the kindergarten teacher, could play the piano and Gerta thought it too good an opportunity to miss. Both kindergarten classes and music lessons were held in a big old house in Orrong Road, set in an old garden with rambling roses and high grass. Margot went there joyfully, clutching Natalie's fat little paw in one hand and her own knitting in the other. Natalie was only eighteen months old, but Gerta thought Miss Shand would be good for her, too. Very often half the stitches of the knitting would be dropped on the way, and Miss Shand would patiently pick them up for the small knitter.

It so happened that about the time Margot's piano lessons were commenced, a dark-haired little boy in another suburb was also starting his. Many years later music was to bring them together and change the pattern of their lives. At the moment the strands were separate, though imperceptibly moving towards their interweaving.

It was a wonderful day when the calipers were removed from Margot's legs.

'Will I have to wear them again?' she asked the doctor.

'No. Never. Never again!'

'And I can run and jump as much as I like?'

'As much as you like. For the rest of your life, my dear.'

'For the rest of my life,' echoed the child solemnly. An incredulous and delighted smile spread over her face. She could hardly wait for the next morning when she could race in to show Miss Shand her beautiful legs.

From kindergarten Margot graduated to Caulfield North State School and thence to the Presbyterian Ladies' College, a school which had staunchly advocated higher education for women at a time when this idea was viewed with suspicion by the general community. Among Old Collegians were such women as social reformer Vida Goldstein, Julia Flynn of the Education Department, author Henry Handel (Ethel) Richardson, and the world-famous singer Dame Nellie Melba.

Margot settled in with the same enthusiasm she brought to everything she did. She came home elated on the first day, and announced that her real name was Margaret, they had called her that in class, and please would the family do the same.

Her head in the clouds, she danced out of the kitchen singing:

'This old man, he played one,
He played knick-knack on my drum,
Knick-knack paddywack give a dog a bone,
This old man came rolling home.'

She sang straight through all ten verses. By the time she came to the end the whole family, from various corners of the house, was singing with her.

All the family loved music, particularly singing, with which they made their generous contribution to school and church choirs. Both boys were to win choir scholarships towards their general education. At Christmas their carol-singing delighted the large circle of friends and relatives who gathered for the Watkins' annual Christmas party. The rooms were lit with candles, the

Christmas tree gleamed in a corner, cards decorated the shelves. And always there was a special time during the evening when, sitting quietly in the candlelight, they listened to the piano-playing of June, the musician of the group. Everybody had his special request to make: Bach, Beethoven, Chopin and Debussy followed each other. The pianist never seemed to tire, for no matter what the hour of day or night, if it were Gerta who asked her to play, June never refused.

As the years flew by the soft faces of the children took on the sensitivity of adolescence, and then the firm features of young adults. Young lovers joined the singers. The cards now numbered hundreds from places all over the world where John and Gerta had travelled, kindling new friendships wherever they went. There might be several babies in baskets tucked away in one of the bedrooms, small children in dressing-gowns standing watching from the circle of someone's arm. Yet year after year the party was invariably as Margaret remembered it: a time for Christmas music, warm hospitality and loving friendship.

Margaret was twelve when she was told there was going to be a new baby in the family. As a child she had accepted each new arrival without much questioning, but with her own gradual initiation into womanhood, the mystery unfolding before her eyes took on new meaning.

When little Josephine arrived, she was welcomed and adored by the whole family. But Margaret was the one who was allowed to handle her as much as she liked. She bathed, powdered, dressed and cuddled her to her heart's content. Sometimes, holding the baby close in her arms, she thought that this was what she wanted most of all when she grew up: babies of her own, lots of them, a huge family.

The new baby was about seven months old when the family left the small house in Dean Avenue with characteristic suddenness. Gerta one day simply abandoned the problem of trying to find space for the ever-increasing flood of trikes, bikes, cots, prams, dressing tables, cupboards, beds and school cases—she went out and found a bigger place to live. It was a large, solidly built old home in Ryeburne Avenue, Hawthorn. There was a large kitchen, verandahs, a room for each of the children, two toilets.

But the children had scarcely unpacked their belongings when they were out of the house again to be boarded temporarily with relatives and friends. John was now Technical Superintendent for Trans-Australia Airlines, and his work involved frequent trips overseas. This time he was to fly to India as specialist member of the government's Air Transport Inquiry Committee, and Gerta was to accompany him. Margaret accepted the situation with tranquillity. By now she was quite used to it.

Gerta was intensely proud of John's career from his early days as an aeronautical engineer to the time when as Director of Engineering he was decorated by the Queen for his services to Australian aviation. But with a nestful of young, vigorous children she found his frequent absences a great trial. She maintained that the general organization of the household needed two people. She also felt that it imposed a strain on any marriage to have frequent long separations when husband and wife would inevitably develop separate instead of mutual interests. It was for this reason as well as her own eagerness for adventure that she was determined to take every opportunity she could to travel with her husband. At first when she was away the children stayed with relatives and friends, but as the family grew bigger she found it more satisfactory to leave a substitute in charge. Sometimes an old friend, Mrs Mackie, came to housekeep, and when Margaret was older she herself took charge of the household. The children never seemed to suffer any ill effects from their parents' absence. Perhaps this was because they were always such a close-knit family. Perhaps again it was because the spirit of independence was developed in them from the time they were born. But undoubtedly one of the greatest factors was that they themselves travelled almost as much as their parents, who believed that experience was the best teacher.

Their home was always bursting at the seams with visiting relatives and friends. Return invitations were just as numerous, and the usual arrangement was that if a child could save his pocket-money or earn enough by holiday jobs to pay his concession fare for some interstate trip, their parents would give him the money for general expenses. With this incentive the young Watkinses roamed far afield from an early age, sometimes alone, sometimes with a brother or sister.

But the best time was when after various separations all were reunited, and adventures were shared in retrospect. Many friends came year after year to see John's colour slides of the countries visited, and admire the fascinating objects the family gradually collected: wood carvings, china, exquisite prints, saris, jewellery. They were interested in everything.

Margaret romped through her school career with scarcely a set-back, although she was undoubtedly less brilliant than doggedly hard-working and conscientious. She gained a fair share of prizes and scholarships, yet found time to take part in all kinds of extra-curricular activities, and to form lasting friendships. With boundless enthusiasm she sang in the school choir, took a leading part in the school play, served on numerous committees, played sport, debated, and studied religion. It was natural that in her last year she should be both Sports Captain of her house and Vice Head Prefect of the school. Her unfailing good humour and commonsense made her a valuable colleague. Many a harassed prefect, agitated by some incident that had occurred in the school, would be soothed and calmed by Margaret's matter-of-fact and practical view of the problem.

Her own personal dilemma, that of her future, was not so easily solved.

'When you have decided, Daddy and I will help you as much as we can,' said Gerta. 'But we have a big family to educate. If you want to go to university you will simply have to win a Commonwealth Scholarship and pay your own way.'

Margaret did want to go to university. What she could not decide was which course to take. Gerta's strong artistic tastes and John's more scientific habits of mind were in her fairly evenly balanced. She could not decide which should take precedence—would it be possible to find a career which combined the two? She found the answer in architecture. To her parents' delight she gained her scholarship and in 1955 enrolled at the University of Melbourne.

Several of the church choir at St Mark's, Camberwell were young students. Margaret, sitting with the altos, was sure that she had sometimes seen one of the basses at the University cafeteria.

'Let's have a drink,' she said cunningly to her girl friend Rosemary next day after their last lecture. They took their malted milks to a table near the counter, where presently a dark-haired young man came to order a milkshake.

Margaret nudged Rosemary. 'Look, isn't he gorgeous?'

'Who? Oh, him . . . well, yes—if you like that type. Do you know him?'

'Sort of—he's in our church choir. We smile at each other occasionally.'

To their delight he caught sight of Margaret and came over to their table.

'Hullo, do you mind if I sit with you? I suppose we ought to know each other, seeing we're in the same choir. My name's John Lester.'

'I'm Margaret Watkins,' she said, and introduced Rosemary.

'Are you going to take part in the church drama group?' he asked her.

'Yes, I love acting. Are you?'

'I'd like to. Depends on rehearsal times. I play the organ a bit and sometimes I have to play at weddings and so on.'

'Oh, are you musical?'

'I suppose you could call it that. Music seems to run in the family. Actually I'm doing engineering. What course are you doing?'

'Architecture.'

'That's interesting. I've got to go. See you on Sunday.'

In the church drama group Margaret found to her delight that she and John were cast in the same play and would have to rehearse together. Every time they met they seemed to discover more interests in common.

'John's taking me to the Trinity College play,' she said one night at dinner.

'When?' asked Natalie and Ian with great interest.

'Tonight,' said Margaret, escaping quickly to her bedroom.

She was not quite ready when she heard the front doorbell ring and an army of young bodies hurtle towards it. She stalked into the living room, torn between her fury at her brothers and sisters, and the funny way her heart always thumped like mad whenever she saw John.

'Hullo, John. This is Natalie, and Ian, and Phillip, and Josephine. Oh, Mum, this is John. Dad—this is John Lester.'

'You've left out the family dog,' said Natalie, and giggled unrepentantly.

'You wait till your turn comes, you little devil,' whispered

24

Margaret as she and John eventually went to the door with seven escorts, the last wagging his tail.

'Have a good time!' chorused six voices. Six pairs of eyes watched as they walked selfconsciously down the steps.

'H'm. Quite a family,' said John. To which Margaret could think of no reply.

Margaret's engagement to John Lester, soon after her twenty-first birthday, was announced at the Melbourne University Commencement Ball when she was in her fourth year and he in his third. John, as President of the Students' Representative Council, was the official host. Magnificent in a borrowed dress suit with a pair of enormous tails, he led forward his new fiancée to receive the plaudits of the crowd, the laughter of the Lord Mayor and a bassinet from his fellow students. The bassinet was complete with woolly toys and plastic baby rattles, and a delightful picture of the whole scene later appeared in *Farrago*, the University student newspaper. Margaret took the joke with her usual good humour —she and John had planned, anyway, to have an enormous family.

Being engaged to John was wonderful, but it brought its problems. They had no money and, as yet, no prospect of buying a house or supporting the family they hoped to have. Both of them were beginning to have trouble in their chosen courses. John, versatile in his interests, had slowly realized that engineering was not for him, yet to change in midstream would place him even further away from his goal of supporting a wife. Margaret, after years of intensive study, suddenly felt she had reached saturation point. In 1959, her final year, she had passed all but two of her exams, and found herself required to design a block of flats. She felt it was temporarily beyond her. It was as if her brain had seized. Her longed-for marriage with John seemed unattainable, the completion of their university degrees just as far off.

After seemingly endless discussions, they found the solution to their problems. Margaret would take a job in an architect's office as soon as possible; John would start work in January as a trainee executive at Containers Ltd, a well-known firm which specialized in the manufacture of different types of packages. They would complete their degrees some time in the future. At present, they decided, the important thing was to be together. With hardly any money, but high hopes for the future they set their wedding date for May, a few months hence.

Meanwhile, they decided to take their last opportunity for a holiday before settling down to a hard year's work. Some of their Melbourne University friends were driving the 400 miles to the Federal Capital for a political science conference to be held in Canberra during the January holiday weekend. Richard McGlashan was taking two or three men in his small car. John and Margaret would borrow his father's sedan, with a student friend, George Hicks, as co-driver with John. Margaret was radiant. All her problems, she felt, had been solved. She looked forward to a future of sheer bliss with the man she loved.

two || THE ACCIDENT

'I'm glad you enjoyed the conference, but it's a pity you can't stay longer. You must come again,' said their hostess, Catherine Blakers, as Margaret wrapped sandwiches for the long drive back to Melbourne.

'Margaret has to be back at work tomorrow, unfortunately, or we could have stayed,' said John Lester. 'My new job doesn't start till next week. Heavens! Look at the time, my girl—we were due to pick up George half an hour ago.' He finished his coffee hurriedly and rose to his feet.

'We've enjoyed every minute,' said Margaret warmly. 'Thanks very much for having us. And thanks for showing us the plans of your new home. Next time I come I'll be able to skite that I've actually stayed in a house designed by the architect of Melbourne's new Cultural Centre, or whatever they decide to call it.'

'You do that,' laughed Catherine.

'A plug for Roy Grounds—not that he needs it,' said John as they went down the front steps. 'Come on, slowcoach.'

'I like that!' exclaimed Margaret indignantly. 'Who's been doing all the work?'

27

'Have a good trip,' called Catherine.

'We will, don't worry!' The two faces were framed for an instant in the car windows, then turned away as the sedan moved off down the hill. Margaret looked back again to wave; her happy smile, so like Gerta's, was the last Catherine saw of them.

George Hicks was waiting for them. Richard, Howard and Bruce had already gone on ahead in Richard's car.

'Who's driving?' asked George as he stowed his gear into the car.

'I'll drive for a hundred miles or so,' said John, 'and then you take over.'

'Right.'

The two young men settled themselves in the front seat, while Margaret spread herself comfortably in the back.

It was a warm, sunshiny afternoon, clear and golden. They left the Federal Capital behind and John drove steadily along the narrow road, through undeveloped bush country where grey-green gum-trees seemed to drowse in the midsummer heat. There was no sign of the others—evidently Richard had made the most of his ten minutes' start. As they neared the Hume Highway, named after one of Australia's early explorers, the bushland gave way to patches of wheat and pasture land. The road joined the highway a few miles out of Yass and now ran on through hills, with sheep grazing on either side. Margaret distributed the sandwiches, eating her own share as she luxuriously curled up on the back seat.

'We should have brought something to drink,' she remarked.

'We'll get a cuppa at Gundagai when we stop for petrol,' said John.

'Where the dog sits on the tuckerbox—wouldn't Jo love to see that!'

She put her head out of the window as they passed the famous statue of the dog faithfully guarding his master's dinner. A few miles later they came into the little country town of Gundagai, where they stopped to refill the car and have afternoon tea.

'Do you want me to take over here?' asked George.

'Might as well. We'll do it in hundred-mile bursts, more or less.'

'I'll sit in the front with George,' said Margaret, 'and you can stretch out in the back.'

They set off again, with George at the wheel. The late afternoon sky was greying a little, and now and then a light shower of rain made the road wet. 'Can't tell if the weather's going to break or not,' said George, when at six o'clock the sun had re-emerged for the third or fourth time.

They had left Holbrook, the centre of a rich pastoral district, and were nearing the border between New South Wales and their own State of Victoria. Albury, the main border town, was twenty-five miles away. The countryside was flat on either side of the road, framed by distant hills, blue in the early evening sunshine.

'Mullengandra coming up,' said George as they approached a curve.

Margaret turned to speak to John and saw that he was stretched out on the back seat with his eyes closed.

'John's fast asleep!' she exclaimed with amusement.

It was the last remark she was to remember of that day. Nobody quite knew how it happened, but a second later the car skidded on the curve, left the road, struck a culvert guardpost and overturned, crashing roof first on to the bank of the dry gully beside the road.

The little boy at the woodheap close to the house down the road heard the frightful crash and rushed indoors calling to his grandfather.

'Grandpa! There's been an accident up at the corner! Can I get your telescope?'

Mr Anderson fetched the telescope and they ran outside to look. His heart sank at what he saw.

'I'll go down and see if I can be of any help. No, son, you can't come with me.' He was in his car and driving down the road before the boy could protest.

In the Royal Oak Hotel at Mullengandra, Vic Gibson, a hairdresser from Holbrook, and Don Dyson, a schoolteacher from Table Top, were finishing their late afternoon drinks with a group of friends when a greyish Volkswagen screeched to a halt outside the hotel. They looked up in surprise as a soldier rushed into the bar, white-faced.

'Quick,' he panted. 'Where can I get an ambulance? There's been a bad accident up at the corner.'

'Holbrook's the nearest—'

29

'No—the Holbrook one hasn't got a driver at the moment. Better try Albury. Phone's out here—'

Several of the men dashed out to the phone with him. The man in the middle of a leisurely conversation about the price of wheat was astonished when several people ran at him, and with a hasty explanation, cut off his call.

'Ask for the Murray Valley District Ambulance Service,' said Don Dyson. 'Exchange will put you through. Tell them it's an emergency.' But the soldier was so shaken with what he had seen that Don took over the phone himself.

'Here, I'll speak to them.' He reported a moment later, 'He says the Albury base sent an ambulance to Holbrook this morning in charge of Officer Stepto. They'll contact him immediately, because Holbrook's nine miles nearer to us than Albury is.'

'Thanks, mate. I'll go back and see if I can do anything—if not, I'd better be on my way back to camp.' He drove off in his Volkswagen as the others raced for their cars.

Over at Holbrook the officer in charge of the police station, Sergeant Hateley, recently posted from Sydney, was at his home when he saw the ambulance being driven at high speed down the main street. He immediately went into the station office and checked with the exchange, whereupon he received the message about the accident. Within a few minutes he was in his car, following the ambulance.

John Lester had not been completely asleep when Margaret made her laughing remark. He heard the murmur of George's reply, although he could not catch the words. A second later came the horrifying crash, chaos, and the numbness of shock. When he recovered his breath, and saw an open buckled door near him, he managed to crawl painfully out with shaking, powerless limbs that seemed not to be his own. A young man lay unconscious on the muddy bank of the culvert—George Hicks, who evidently had been flung out of the driver's seat.

'Margaret!' thought John. She was nowhere to be seen. She had been in the seat next to the driver. He scrabbled frantically around the crushed car—then saw her, a crumpled heap pinned underneath the wreckage. 'She's gone,' he thought. Still too shocked to register anything except the need to find help for his friends, he staggered somehow on to the road in spite of the searing pain in his back. A soldier in a Volkswagen slowed down in horror at the scene.

'Get help . . . ambulance . . . doctor . . .' muttered John.

Another motorist was already pulling up to offer assistance. Seeing that John would not be alone, the soldier sped off towards the Royal Oak Hotel to give the alarm.

By the time the ambulance and police arrived, a small crowd had already gathered at the scene. A young man who had been one of the first to arrive had managed to crawl close enough to Margaret's shattered body to draw her head on to his lap. He sat holding her, murmuring words of comfort into her semi-conscious ears, while others tried to give first aid to the two young men. George, by this time, was conscious and in great pain.

Officer Stepto made a brief examination as best he could.

'Leave me alone,' muttered Margaret thickly. Her voice trailed off as she lapsed into coma; her breathing became shallow and irregular.

Stepto exchanged a glance with Sergeant Hateley. 'She's so far gone I wouldn't give much for her chances,' he said quietly.

'Better cut inquiries short until we get them all into hospital, then.'

'Yes. How to extricate her from under this mess of metal, that's the problem. Moving her isn't going to do her any good. Could you start figuring it out while I have a quick look at the men?'

A big man in shorts moved closer to the Sergeant. 'Can I help you?' Several other people, including the group from the hotel, volunteered their services.

'Thanks. We'll need some strength. We'll have to work with the ambulance officer, though, so as not to injure the girl any further.'

Officer Stepto returned. A light drizzling rain had begun to fall again. 'Looks as if both the men have injured spines. We've made them as comfortable as we can. Pity about the rain—well, it's not too heavy, thank goodness. They can travel in the top two berths of the ambulance and the lass can go in a bottom one—when we get her out. Now, let's see.' He glanced at Margaret's face, and bent down to examine her again.

'She's out to it, so fortunately she won't know what's going on,' said the Sergeant. 'If you can keep holding her head steady,' he added, turning to the young man, 'we'll get some of this junk off her before we try to move her. It's still broad daylight, thank goodness. I wouldn't care to do this at night. No thanks,' to Mr Anderson, who had come forward. 'I think we've got enough volunteers for this job. But I'd be grateful if you'd collect all the personal belongings that are scattered about, and hang on to them till I pick them up later.' Mr Anderson nodded and started to gather up the possessions that lay pathetically strewn in and about the shattered car—briefcases, hand luggage, a compact, sunglasses, a purse, two or three books. Several people silently helped him. It was a relief to be given even the smallest task when there was nothing they could do directly to help the pretty young girl who lay trapped and shockingly injured.

It took them half an hour to free Margaret from the wreckage. They worked frantically as her breathing and pulse deteriorated, but nevertheless they were forced to proceed slowly lest they do worse harm. It seemed an eternity to all before at last she was free and, under Officer Stepto's careful instructions, was lifted on to a stretcher.

John, already lying in the top compartment, heard them slide her stretcher into the back of the ambulance. He knew now that she was still alive, although only just.

'You'll be all right now, dear,' he said comfortingly.

But Margaret was beyond hearing.

'Full speed ahead for Albury Base Hospital,' said Officer Stepto, swinging into the driver's seat and starting the screaming siren.

'I'll follow you in the police car and I'll stop at Bowna to alert the hospital,' said the Sergeant.

They speeded off to the eerie wail of the siren, watched by the people who had so willingly helped the victims. After a while the helpers went to their own cars and drove away, still shaken by what they had experienced.

Subsequently John and Gerta Watkins went to much trouble to find and thank all who had helped the victims of the accident. Most were easily located. But a few—the soldier, the man in shorts, and the young man who held Margaret's head in his lap—they never succeeded in finding, in spite of their efforts. Perhaps, John Watkins hoped, they might read the letter published in the *Border Morning Mail* in which he and Gerta publicly expressed their gratitude.

Photo by John Watkins copied by Fred Cropley

Margaret Anne, three years old

John Watkins

Margaret in her teens, dancing on the beach with Natalie

'Mum, aren't you going to drink your coffee before you go?' called Natalie from the kitchen.

'Bring it in, darling, will you?' answered Gerta from the bedroom. 'Daddy's gone out to the car already—we mustn't be late for the theatre. And Nonnie and Grandpa Carey will be waiting.'

She was rapidly dabbing French perfume on herself as she spoke, clasping a great copper bracelet around her wrist, and pinning on a striking brooch. No one else could wear jewellery the way she did. The most outrageous combinations of hand-wrought metal and flamboyant costume jewellery looked exactly right on Gerta; anyone else would have stripped them off in despair after one glance in the mirror. She added an improbable scarf and snatched a light evening wrap from the wardrobe.

'There! How do I look?'

'Fabulous—here, drink your coffee.'

Gerta took one scalding gulp, dumped the steaming Swedish mug on to the dressing table, and bounced out of the house. She bounced back again to hug Natalie. 'Goodbye, darling. Have a happy time getting ready for school tomorrow. You too, Ian! You can help each other.' She gave her deep chuckle and fled in the direction of John Watkins' resigned tooting.

'You know, I don't think Mum will ever really grow up,' sighed Natalie, rescuing the Swedish mug and taking it back to the kitchen.

'Happy time is right,' grunted Ian, following her. His Scotch College classes started next day; at the same time Natalie was to commence her first job, teaching art and crafts at a girls' secondary school. They looked at each other gloomily.

'Who's going to help who?' asked Natalie ungrammatically.

'You come and help me sort out my books and then I'll help you sort out yours,' invited Ian.

'Done,' said his sister. She assisted him for over an hour by sitting on his bed and giggling while he pulled all his books out of the cupboard, arranged them in a slightly different order and stuffed them back again.

'It's nearly time for you to help me,' she said as the phone rang in the kitchen. 'Are you going to answer that?'

'No, you answer it.'

They argued amiably as they set off to the kitchen together. Natalie reached the phone first.

33

'It's trunks,' she informed him, waiting for the caller to be put through. A man's voice came on the other end, impersonally kind, definite, urgent. Natalie listened . . . shock crept throughout her system, her face grew whiter and whiter, she was unable to speak.

'What is it? Who is it?' demanded Ian. He reached over and took the phone away from her shaking hands.

'This is Ian Watkins—'

'Albury police here—' The voice repeated the urgent message.

'All right,' Ian said. He replaced the receiver and put his arm around Natalie who was shaking all over. 'Come on,' he said, 'we've got to get Mum and Dad up to Albury—' He stopped himself from adding 'before it's too late'. 'What theatre are they at? The Princess? The Comedy? I know, I think Uncle John Carey bought the tickets—he'll know where they're sitting. I'll ring him.'

John Carey was at home. He said at once that he would go to the theatre and tell John and Gerta himself.

'Will they go straight to Albury?' asked Natalie at last.

'I think they'll come home for money and warm clothes and things. Make some coffee, Nat—and sandwiches for them to take. What about some thermoses?' He kept thinking of things she could do, anything to bring her out of her white-faced shock.

Natalie did as she was told, like someone in a dream. Presently they heard the car outside, and Gerta came into the kitchen.

'She isn't young any more,' thought Natalie, looking up at the face of a stricken, old woman, and she was filled with terror. Her mother put her arms around her.

'It's all right, Nat. Daddy and I are going to get her. Come and help me change.'

Within minutes they were off again, with Phillip, to pick up John Lester's father, Theo; then on their two-hundred-mile race against time to Albury and District Base Hospital. They arrived there at three in the morning.

Looking at the almost unrecognizable, deeply unconscious figure in the hospital bed, Gerta went over and over in her mind the terrible list of injuries. She could not see how Margaret could live, but she continued to pray. Margaret's chest had been crushed, causing broken ribs, bruising of the left lung and haemorrhage into the chest cavity; she had severe concussion, a fractured jaw, bruises and lacerations all over her body, and was badly shocked. But most ominous of all were the words of the matron: 'I haven't yet seen her move her legs at all, and I don't like the look of it. We shall know more after some X-rays have been taken.'

The X-rays were taken at midday; later in the afternoon the doctor gave his report to John Watkins. Margaret had a severe fracture-dislocation of the upper part of the thoracic spine, which had damaged her spinal cord and paralysed her below the chest. It could not yet be established whether the spinal cord were actually severed. If this were so, her paralysis would be permanent.

'What does it mean? What can we do? asked Gerta when she and John were alone together. She looked at him appealingly— she knew from long experience that John's resourcefulness and determination would show them the best way of coping with the situation, no matter how desperate it seemed.

He said after a moment's thought, 'There must be doctors who specialize in such cases. I think we should find out who is the best man in Victoria and get her into his care as soon as possible. I'll make some inquiries.'

He rang a medical friend in Melbourne and was given the information he required. He came back to tell Gerta that the best place for Margaret was undoubtedly the Spinal Injuries Centre at the Austin Hospital in the Melbourne suburb of Heidelberg. It was directed by an English doctor called David Cheshire, who had trained at Stoke Mandeville under Dr Ludwig Guttmann.*

The names meant nothing to Gerta.

'It's the State centre for severe spinal cases,' added John, to reassure her.

'Can we get her in?'

'They have a vacant bed and will keep it for her.'

The doctor agreed that the Spinal Injuries Centre offered the best possible treatment, but said that Margaret was far too ill to be moved immediately. 'A two-hundred-mile trip in her condition —it's unthinkable.'

'Even in an ambulance?'

The doctor shook his head. 'Most inadvisable.'

But John, once set on what he believed to be the right course, never gave up. He himself spoke to the officers of the Murray

---

* Now Sir Ludwig Guttmann.

Valley District Ambulance Service; as a result the chief officer came personally to see the doctor and assured him that he would drive the vehicle himself, with all possible care.

Early in the afternoon of the following day, Margaret, still unconscious and in a desperate condition, was driven the two hundred miles to Melbourne. John Watkins followed the ambulance in his car, marvelling at the superb driving of the man in front, who changed from dead slow to seventy-five miles an hour according to the state of the road, so that his patient received never a jolt. Theo Lester and Phillip Watkins had already returned by train. Both John Lester and George Hicks had suffered fractures of the spine, but fortunately without damage to the spinal cord. They were to be transferred to the Royal Melbourne Hospital by ambulance the following day.

'At least two of them will be all right eventually,' thought Gerta. Sitting in the ambulance beside Margaret she scarcely took her eyes off the greenish, waxen face of her daughter; at times she imagined that the faint breathing had stopped, and bent forward desperately to listen.

They passed through Melbourne and arrived at the Austin Hospital at twenty past seven in the evening. A team of people instantly took possession of Margaret's still figure and bore it away.

'Wait here, please, while they settle her into the ward,' said Dr Cheshire.

'Will we be able to see her? When are the visiting hours? When can we come?' asked Gerta. She could not bear the separation.

'Whenever you like,' he replied. 'Any hour of the day. Or night.'

three || ACUTE WARD

'The universe,' thought Margaret hazily, 'is a chaos of pain. . . . The worlds that make up the universe, I've got to learn them off by heart, but they won't keep still long enough. There's one world in my chest—that's the worst. It's all pain. It can't be the whole world, though. Because there's another world in my head and that's turning all the time. It might stop hurting if it would keep still. There's a separate world in my mouth. That hurts as much as the one in my chest, but it doesn't whirl quite so fast. I'll be all right so long as they don't crash into each other.'

But hands came out of darkness and seized her naked body. All the worlds whirled crazily out of control, the whole universe spun in unbearable pain. She tried to scream wildly that they must leave her alone before all the spinning worlds crashed into each other hurling her into eternity, but the words came out only as hoarse sounds.

A voice said, 'It's all right, darling. It will make you feel so much better.'

Then there was, after all, pattern and order and design in the universe. With a sigh Margaret slipped back thankfully into the world she had always known, the one of security and love. She opened her eyes, as she had known she would, on Gerta's smiling face.

Her father's voice came to her. 'Margaret?'

'Come farther down here so that she can see you, John.'

His face came into view, wavered and dissolved again. Margaret tried to speak, but there was no response from her muscles. She did not know that her jaw had been fractured—it seemed too great an effort for her to move her mouth.

'Your mouth feels a bit funny,' Gerta reassured her. 'It'll be all right soon.'

'Where am I?' she tried to croak.

'You're in bed, darling. There was a car accident. You'll have to rest up for a while.'

'An accident?' Margaret's eyes showed her astonishment.

'Don't you remember?' asked her father. Her blank face told him that she remembered nothing.

John and Gerta exchanged glances.

'I think her mind is functioning,' he said quietly, 'even though she doesn't remember the accident itself.' The word 'body' flashed unspoken between them as they looked down at the still—so unnaturally still—figure on the bed. From under the sheet that covered Margaret from chest to ankles two motionless feet protruded, still with gaily painted red toenails. The bare shoulders and long bandaged arms lay stretched over the white cotton sheet.

'I'm pretty sure her arms are all right,' whispered John, gently squeezing the hand nearest to him. Margaret's eyes opened instantly. She looked from one hand to the other and dismay roused her.

'Where is it?' she croaked.

'What's the matter, darling?' asked Gerta.

'My engagement ring. It's gone!'

John reassured her. 'It's safe. The Sister is keeping it for you.' He did not tell her that it had been taken off her finger during the X-rays.

'Can't I have it?'

'I'll ask Sister right away.'

Something was worrying Margaret. Somebody she loved very much who wasn't there—where was he? Before she could form the question, the pain in her chest became so intense that all else blurred in her mind. Someone was pushing a needle into her arm

. . . she was drifting off again . . . Gerta's voice was gently soothing her. Everything faded.

And then, almost instantly it seemed, the hands were clutching again at her bare body. The pain was unbearable.

'Steady,' said a man's voice.

'Can't you leave me alone?'

'No, my dear. That's just what we can't do . . . there.'

Whatever they had done to her had started the planets of pain off again into their mad dance.

'That's to make you feel better,' said the familiar, loving voice. 'Have a little sleep now.'

The mad rhythm slowed down, faltered, and ceased. She was drifting off into unconsciousness when an image that had been forming vaguely in her mind suddenly came sharply into focus. It jerked her into full consciousness.

'John! Where's John?'

'John's all right.'

'Why isn't he here?'

'He hurt his back and he's in hospital, but he's going to be quite all right before long. He sent you a letter. Shall I hold it so that you can read it?'

It was a brief, loving message scrawled in John's unmistakable hand and it reassured her more than any verbal message could have done.

'Could you get me some paper and a pencil so that I can answer it?'

'Of course. Have a little rest while I see if they've got any at the kiosk.'

Before she was out of the ward Margaret was asleep.

Blessed with the marvellous recuperative powers of youth and health, Margaret's body gradually began to mend. As she returned to full consciousness she began to take an interest in her surroundings. She found to her astonishment that many things she had thought to be dreams were in fact true. She *was* completely naked under the sheet; the forest of male hands that had seemed to materialize out of the air belonged to a flesh-and-blood team of men who came at regular hours to turn her—side, back, side—directed by the Sister. At first she dreaded their coming, every two hours, all day and all night. But she soon realized, without understanding why, that she was unable to ease herself into a more comfortable position. In fact, when the pain became unbearable she often found herself calling out, and asking over and over again when the team was due. When they came they lifted and turned her with expert gentleness; she supposed that exhaustion was what prevented her from using her own muscles to help them.

Moreover, there were men in bed in the same ward, and they also were stark naked, as she saw to their mutual embarrassment one day when someone hurried in and pulled off a patient's sheet without remembering to close the cubicle curtains. Later she learnt the reason the patients wore no clothes. It was because, acutely ill as they were, they required constant attention and highly specialized nursing; continual dressing and undressing would be both time-consuming for the nurses and a nuisance to the patient. Moreover, the turning teams' powdered hands could manage a badly injured body with greater skill if there were no garments to slip and slide. Nor must the patient ever lie on rumpled clothes that might cause dangerous pressure against the unfeeling skin. Margaret could see only the one man beside her when she was lying on one side; on the other side were the windows. Through them she could see patches of sky, tree-tops, and sometimes the roofs of passing cars. She was conscious of other personalities in the ward, perhaps eight or nine, but at present they were only voices that called to each other. One man moaned continuously. Another cursed and swore violently, using language she had never heard before, until someone went to him and told him he must stop. One of the voices was a woman's.

Around and among the still figures, each draped with a single sheet, people moved quietly and incessantly, caring for their needs. Sisters, nurses, doctors came and went continually. The turning team moved from one bed to another. Visitors came at any hour of the day. Sometimes they brought flowers: Margaret received her full share. A nurse would give her one tantalizing glimpse of roses or carnations; she might be allowed to hold them for a few minutes and bury her face in their fragrance. But almost immediately the card would be detached, and the flowers whisked away behind the glass observation window. With turning teams and so many other people moving swiftly about, vases of flowers would simply be in the way, explained Sister Gillings who was in charge of the ward.

Margaret was rather in awe of Sister Gillings. She was a tall, dark-haired young woman, with a round, pleasant face, and eyes that smiled kindly behind her glasses. But like the Director, Dr Cheshire, she was a perfectionist, both by nature and because of her tremendous faith in his ability to conduct a first-class spinal centre. 'We must do what Dr Cheshire says,' she would say to any patient who might croak a faint protest at some treatment that had been ordered for his benefit. Or, if something were less than perfectly done, 'You can't have second-best. We can't take any chances.' Nevertheless, with all the responsibility she carried, she found time to talk personally with every patient in her care; and no matter how many flowers Margaret received, Sister Gillings made sure that every bouquet took its turn in the place of honour behind the observation window, where Margaret could just see it.

A totally different character was Sister O'Dwyer, a cheerful and sprightly Irish girl who was expert at the bantering repartee which helped to keep the patients cheerful. There was a male nurse, too: Mr Taylor, a handsome and courteous young man who was greatly admired by the female staff, especially since most of them were remarkably young.

Gradually Margaret learnt to know and appreciate them all as they went about their appointed tasks, which were co-ordinated by the Director, a tall, youthful-looking Englishman, whose tremendous vitality and drive made itself felt throughout the entire Spinal Centre. Whenever Dr Cheshire entered the ward, Margaret recognized his decisive walk even before he came into her line of vision, his lively eyes missing no detail. She was to appreciate him fully in the days to come.

Gerta brought notepaper. In a faint, spidery scrawl Margaret managed to pencil: 'John, I'm thinking of you. Heaps of love.' It was enough for him, lying immobilized on a specially shaped bed in the Royal Melbourne Hospital, worrying ceaselessly about her. He wrote back immediately, reassuring her that his own spinal injury was making good progress. He hoped to be off his back before too long. George Hicks, too, was gradually recovering.

Margaret replied that she didn't know when she'd be off *her* back; it could take twelve weeks. She also told him that she'd discovered her jaw was fractured and that three teeth were missing.

41

He wrote back immediately to comfort her. In fact he wrote every day, telling her cheerful inconsequential details of his life in hospital, enclosing crossword puzzles to keep her amused, telling her of the books he was reading.

Margaret lived for his letters.

'I've put my big photo of you on the locker next to my bed,' she scrawled awkwardly. 'It's fun being in a ward with men, with all the moaning and groaning and jokes that go on. I'm still being fed. They keep sticking pins into me. But I can't feel them yet.'

It often happens that a person faced with disaster instinctively knows what has happened for quite some time before it is acknowledged by the conscious mind.

It would be difficult to say exactly when Margaret became aware of the unnatural stillness of her own body. There was no sudden shock of revelation, merely a gradual realization of a curious lack of sensation below chest level.

'How are you today, Margaret?' Dr Cheshire bent over her to catch her reply.

'I'm fine, thank you, but do you know, I think there might be something wrong with my legs. Do you think perhaps you should look at them?'

'You know you've been in a car accident, Margaret?'

'Yes, but I didn't know my legs had been hurt. I don't feel any pain in them. I just can't move them, that's all. Is anything wrong there?'

'You can't move them because your spine was fractured in the accident, and it looks as if your spinal cord was damaged. That means that although your legs weren't hurt, no messages can get *to* them from your brain—or *from* them back to your brain.'

Margaret was silent.

'I think perhaps you'd guessed that yourself, hadn't you?'

'Well, sort of. But that means—that means I won't be able to walk any more.'

'Yes. Unless the cord heals itself. We can't tell yet for sure.' He looked straight into her shocked eyes. 'There is a slight chance that it may heal—if so, you will recover full use of your legs. We shall know in about six weeks. But I must warn you that the chance is very slight indeed.' He paused, and then continued: 'I know what a great shock this is to you, but you must believe,

Margaret, that life is not ended when a person can't walk any more. You are young and strong—there will be many things you *will* be able to do to live a full and useful life. You still have the use of your arms and hands, you know.'

Margaret's fingers closed around the engagement ring that her father had put back on her finger.

'The only thing I want to do is get married,' she said, 'but I guess I'd better send this back.'

'I wouldn't do that if I were you.'

'But what use will I be—?'

'You could be a lot of use, Margaret.'

'But if I couldn't have children—'

'Nobody said you couldn't have children. Fortunately, as far as we can judge there's been no damage to any internal organs —except your lung, of course. Take my advice and just wait a little while. Don't break off your engagement. This is the man's business, not yours.' He went on quietly explaining the details of her injuries. Why there was loss of feeling and power in the trunk. Why there was no longer any control of the body's natural functions.

When he had gone Margaret lay staring at the windows. In a shaft of sunlight motes were dancing purposelessly, like the images that were whirling round in her mind. She saw herself riding the sixteen-foot surfboard at Lorne, soaring triumphantly over the roaring breakers. She remembered the long hikes through the bush and up the mountains into the snow, the never-to-be-forgotten thrill of whizzing down the slopes on skis. She thought of her feet that she'd always taken for granted, moving heedlessly between bedroom, bathroom and toilet, hurrying to the tram, driving the car, walking into a university lecture room, in and out of shops.

'How can I do all these things now?' she thought. 'What use would I be as a wife? I couldn't even cook a meal or peg out the washing. What on earth am I going to do? How will I manage?'

Gerta came hurrying into the ward.

'Darling, I've brought you lots of tomato juice—look! Would you like some straight away? I've got that thing to pierce the tin with!' She poured some into a spoon and began gently to feed Margaret, taking great care not to hurt the broken jaw.

Margaret drank gratefully. She had to concentrate very hard.

It wasn't easy to drink lying flat on one's back, with a broken jaw. The intravenous feeding had been stopped, and she was beginning to feel hungry, but she could still take nothing by mouth except thin liquids.

Gerta glanced at the unopened chocolates on the locker.

'Once they've fixed your jaw you'll be able to eat properly,' she said. 'Doctor says he doesn't think there'll be any scars at all on the outside. Isn't that lucky, darling? You'll look exactly the same.'

Margaret's heart was filled with concern. She still had to break the news to her parents. It had to be done.

'Mum,' she said when she'd finished the juice, 'I've got some bad news for you. About my legs.'

'I think I know, darling. But they can still get better, you know. Let's not worry about it just now.'

'I've got to worry about it,' said Margaret. 'Because of John. I'm sure he won't want to marry me if I can't walk.'

'How can you be sure?' replied Gerta quietly. 'You can't tell how he'll feel about it.'

'I wish I could see him. I wish I knew how he was.'

'He's all right, really he is. He just has to stay in bed for a few weeks, that's all.'

'What's *wrong* with him? No one will tell me exactly.'

'He's fractured his spine, but not too badly. The doctors are very pleased with him.'

'Don't you think I should break off our engagement?'

'No, I don't. That's John's business. Anyway let's just wait, and hope that you'll get better.'

'Mum, I want you to do something for me. Will you break the news to Dad—it'll be awful for him. Tell him not to worry. I'll be all right. I've still got my arms and hands. There are lots of things I'll be able to do, Dr Cheshire says.'

Gerta turned away to hide her tears.

'Will you give me my writing paper and pencil?' Margaret asked.

Gerta found the notepaper printed 'Dial M for Margaret' that had made them all laugh at Christmas time—an eternity ago.

'I've got to tell John. I think if I drew a sketch I could explain it better.' She drew a sketch of herself lying in bed. 'This is me,' she wrote under it. 'The fracture is high up, I've marked it with a cross. T4 + T5 it's called, that means the 4th and 5th thoracic vertebrae. I can't move or feel *anything* below the fracture.'

Gerta took the note away, and for weeks Margaret anxiously scanned John's daily letters to see how he would comment on the sketch.

He never mentioned it.

If Margaret had thought the endless regular turnings comprised a routine that never gave her any peace, she was soon to find that they were almost restful compared with the planned activity that now began to build up between the turnings.

One day two young girls in white coats came briskly into the ward. One paused and looked down in surprise at the scratched face of the new patient.

'Haven't I seen you before?'

Margaret tried to nod. 'At the ski club. Elspeth McColl, isn't it? Do you work here?'

'I'm one of the physiotherapists. And this is Jenny Sanders, who will be looking after you.' Elspeth tried to hide her dismay. It was her first encounter with a badly injured patient whom she had known personally.

She moved away as Jenny smiled at Margaret. 'I'm here to put you through your exercises.'

'Exercises!' croaked Margaret. 'I can't even move yet.'

'I know—that's why they're all the more important. We have to keep those legs supple to prevent contractures.' She turned back the sheet and began to bend and straighten Margaret's unresisting lower limbs. Margaret watched with interest. Jenny was a quiet, capable-looking girl who inspired confidence, but it seemed queer to Margaret to see her legs moving at someone else's will instead of her own.

'When I look down I can always see my feet sticking out from under the sheet,' she observed. 'Why don't they cover them up?'

'I expect it's so Sister can keep an eye on their colour. It's very important that good circulation be maintained. If your feet are exposed she can see at a glance what's going on. Now I want you to do some breathing exercises for that collapsed lung.' These were painful at first, but the patient co-operated as well as she could. No sooner had she mastered these than Jenny announced a new series for strengthening arms and back.

'Your arms will have to develop double strength, Margaret, because from now on you're going to have to rely on them for everything you do. Yes, you *can* do them lying down. Come on, I'll show you. Right arm first.'

The exercises were a daily routine. Margaret was able to cope alone with those for the upper part of her body. She did them earnestly with great concentration. In her mind a glimmer of light was beginning to appear; for the first time she began to see some sort of pattern in the new life ahead. But just as the agonizing pain in her chest was beginning to subside, there was a new ordeal for her. A dental surgeon, Dr Mills, came one day with an assistant to wire her broken jaw together. Once the unpleasant operation was over, her pain and nervousness subsided, but now, instead of a slack mouth, her teeth were so tightly wired together that the only way she could take nourishment was to suck in liquids through a flattened plastic straw which somebody had to wedge between her teeth. Hungrier every day, she pushed the tantalizing chocolates away and propped John's photograph in front of them. Dr Mills, a kindly, fatherly man, came regularly to check progress. He was very interested in the architectural work she described between clenched teeth—once or twice he lent some books that he thought might interest her.

A few days after the jaw operation two nurses seized her bed and began to push it into a new position in the ward.

'Hey, what's happening?'

'You're being upgraded, that's what. Progress! Sister Gillings's orders!'

'Really?'

'Really. Patients are moved down the ward as their condition improves. Didn't you know? You aren't Number One any more.'

This news pleased Margaret immensely. She was even more delighted when she found a mirror fixed over her bed. Now, instead of a patch of sky and the man in the next bed, she could see people moving about outside as they crunched along the paths between the wards, or went in and out of the kiosk. Sometimes there was a patient in a wheelchair. There was a big grey-green gum-tree, too—that must be where the kookaburras sat when they gave their raucous laughing calls in the early mornings. In her new position she found herself near the only other woman in the ward. This was Mrs Mac, a salty, middle-aged character who,

46

although paralysed in all four limbs, was the one who did most to keep up the general morale of the ward.

'How do you like your new position, Margaret?' asked Dr Cheshire. Accompanied by a senior and junior doctor, he was doing his regular round of the ward, with Sister Gillings in attendance.

'Very much, thank you.'

'Can you feel what I am doing?'

Margaret looked down swiftly. She saw that while talking he was systematically pricking her legs and trunk with a pin. But for the evidence of her eyes she would not have known.

'Can you feel this? This? This?'

She strained, willing herself to sensation, but there was nothing.

'Can you move your toes?'

Margaret mentally wiggled and wriggled her toes, willing them to move, but she did not dare look to see if the red-painted toenails were moving. Instead she asked the doctor, 'Are they moving?'

'No, Margaret. Tell me, can you feel this?'

A faint stirring, as of a moth fluttering over her skin.

'Yes, I can. I can!'

She wrote excitedly to John. 'He rubbed a piece of cotton wool over my leg and I *felt* it. It's the first step to recovering full feeling.'

Excitement brought colour to her face and renewed her hopes. She asked for her vanity case. Gerta brought lipstick and nail varnish. A nurse managed to wash her hair, in spite of all the difficulties, and brought a little bowl of ammonia and water to clean the diamond in her engagement ring. Nothing was too much trouble for the staff: they cared for each helpless patient as a mother for her sick child. Yet there was no babying—on the contrary, a constant encouragement towards the next slow step forward. A friend who was being married sent her wedding bouquet to Margaret. This time she was allowed to keep the flowers longer than the usual few minutes.

'Every patient needs an incentive,' said Sister Gillings to Gerta a few days later. 'Margaret's picture of her fiancé is hers.'

'Do you think this slight sensation in her legs means anything?'

'You'd have to discuss that with Dr Cheshire,' said Sister Gillings instantly.

'She's looking so much better,' said Gerta hopefully.

Sister Gillings hesitated and then said, 'Actually, I'm afraid she's had a poor night. These patients are so liable to bladder infections. She's not feeling quite so well today.'

Hurrying into the ward, Gerta found Margaret feverish and unhappy, her head aching. For three days she felt ill and wretched, then the infection subsided as suddenly as it had developed. As she lay on her side, her head feeling feathery and dizzy, she stretched her arm down and tried to brush her fingers across the skin the way the doctor had tested with the cottonwool. Did she or did she not feel anything? She was too honest to pretend even to herself. The faint response was like a whisper imagined rather than heard. Neither more nor less audible than before, it was unaccompanied by the slightest ability to move.

Dr Mills came a few days later to take out the wiring of her upper jaw. He expressed mock dismay at all the paraphernalia of spinal nursing among which he had to work, which was further complicated by the blood transfusion Dr Cheshire had ordered for his patient. Overhead dangled a fantastic mobile of coloured cardboard fish sent by the proprietress of Décor Gifts, a shop in Burke Road where Margaret had worked on Saturday mornings. Yellow, red, blue, white and black, they danced and spun in the slightest current of air.

'Now,' said fatherly Dr Mills, when the splint was off, 'you can celebrate by eating some ice-cream. And you should be able to manage some solid food if it's finely minced. Next week we'll take off the lower splint, and by the time we've attended to those missing teeth you'll be up to a real dinner!'

It sounded wonderful, but it had its disadvantages. The strict rule was that no patient was allowed to have anything done for him that he could manage for himself. The days of being fed thin liquids with a straw were over. Soups, custards, or fine minces Margaret had to manage as best she could lying down, guiding the spoon to her mouth by watching her face in the reflector. It was no help to read John's account of how he was being hand-fed by pretty nurses. The drinking of liquids, again without help, was the most difficult. She had to drink at least once an hour to help the natural drainage of the body, and prevent the dreaded infections that in the past had taken the life of so many people with spinal injuries. It was an effort to swallow the necessary amount of

Photos by John Watkins

Two snapshots from the 'fifties: a youthful Margaret with the author, sailing on Albert Park Lake; and the Watkins family about 1957. *Back row (left to right)*: Natalie, Margaret, Gerta, John; *front row*: Ian, Phillip, Josephine

Farrago, University of Melbourne

Margaret and John announce their engagement at the University Commencement Ball and are presented with a bassinet

fluid. But there was a further surprise in store for her. It came a few mornings later.

Outside the window a pair of kookaburras had been laughing raucously in the gum-tree. A truckload of men drove up noisily; as they passed across Margaret's reflector she saw that it was a team from Whelan the Wrecker, a well-known firm specializing in pulling down old buildings. She wondered idly what they were doing at the hospital. They passed tantalizingly out of view and the birds flew off screaming. Margaret turned her head to see Sister O'Dwyer with an enormous jug of water.

'New method for preventing bladder infections,' she was informed. 'Every patient has to drink five pints of water first thing in the morning.'

'Oh, no!'

'Oh, yes. And I've got to see that you do, so start drinking, there's a good girl.'

Margaret started, undeterred by the ribald comments of the patients in the neighbouring beds. 'Your turn will come next,' she assured them between gulps. At the end of the second pint she baulked.

'Three to go,' said Sister O'Dwyer encouragingly. 'Come on, there's a good girl. Show them what you can do.'

Margaret shook her head. She had reached her limit, and no amount of coaxing would induce her to exceed it. A few days later the required intake was mercifully reduced to three pints. Try as she might, however, she never succeeded in getting down more than two.

It was now time for the repair work on her mouth to be finished. The broken jaw had healed, all the wires had been removed, and she found herself able to speak clearly once more. She had graduated from intravenous feeding to thin liquids through a flattened straw, then messy gruels and custards. Only one more ordeal remained for her mouth. The teeth that had been knocked out had to be replaced. For this Dr Mills had to make a wax impression of her mouth. In spite of his kindly reassurances, Margaret, lying on her back, went through terrible panic lest he drop the softened wax down her throat. She need not have worried.

Looking in her mirror, she eventually saw the same familiar face of the days before the accident, and told herself she had been very lucky. At the Communion service, given in the ward for those patients who desired it, she gave heart-felt thanks that her life had been spared. She rediscovered the joy of eating, of chewing good, solid food; and, as she continued to eat, a surge of returning vitality jerked her out of her passive acceptance of the hospital routine. Suddenly she felt she could not endure it for one more day. 'I want to get up and go!' she told Sister Gillings impatiently.

'Some day you will,' promised Sister.

'When will it be?'

'When you've learnt to be completely independent.'

Margaret thought of the incessant activities of everyday life. She couldn't even put a foot out of bed, let alone dress or toilet herself. How on earth could she ever be completely independent? Yet she knew that she would not be prepared to marry John on any other terms. What John thought, she had no way of telling. He continued to avoid the subject.

four ||| THE DEADLINE

As the six weeks crept by and there was no sign of movement in the bare young body under the sheet, Gerta's heart sank lower and lower. Margaret became very quiet during that waiting time. Neither she nor her mother referred again to what was uppermost in their minds. Only Margaret wrote constantly to John Lester with minute descriptions of her condition, and he replied as usual with inconsequential chatter about life in hospital.

'It was wonderful being fed by pretty nurses,' he scribbled. 'Quite the best part of hospital life. Now they are making me feed myself. Such a pity.'

Margaret would come near to despair after reading such a letter. If only he would tell her a little of what was in his mind. How could he continue to ignore so deliberately the one great issue that must be settled, one way or the other?

The deadline came and passed and still they all waited.

Gerta's natural hopefulness was almost completely defeated. She found it harder and harder to keep the cheerful face she always presented to the ward. Sometimes looking around at the patients, many of them young and some in even worse condition than Margaret, a feeling of futility and despair would almost overcome her. She was more tired than she realized, and frequentiy very unwell. John Watkins was ill, which was an added worry. But it was not her habit to give in. The kiosk was nearby. Hot strong black coffee was always available. She lived on it for months.

She was sipping coffee with her sister, Margaret Jensen, who came weekly from Yallourn to be with her, when a young nurse put her head around the door of the kiosk.

'Mrs Watkins? Dr Cheshire would like to see you.'

'This is it,' said Gerta.

She was back fifteen minutes later. Margaret Jensen took one glance at her face and quietly ordered fresh coffee.

'Are you quite sure?' she kept asking Gerta. 'Are you quite *sure*? Do you think they could have made a mistake?'

'She will never walk again, but the doctor says there is hope for her to lead a reasonable life.'

Neither of them was experienced enough in paraplegia to dare to define the limits of the term 'reasonable'. Gerta's tears ran down her cheeks and mingled with the bitter coffee.

John Lester's letters continued to make no reference to Margaret's condition. He seemed to be more interested in describing his own experiences. He was still stretched out in bed, forbidden even to raise his head. A note one day commented that they were going to try the experiment of letting him sit up. But even if it were successful he was likely to be in hospital for a few more weeks yet.

The news depressed Margaret, who had been hoping to see him soon, but she tried to respond cheerfully to the visitors who were laughing and talking around her bed. A fellow architecture student, Jeff Turnbull, had brought some colour slides of his recent visit to South-east Asia, and several of her friends were wrangling amicably over the slide viewer.

In the reflector she observed Sister O'Dwyer coming towards her at top speed.

'*Now* what? They're always doing *something* to me,' she murmured with mock dismay.

Sister was straightening the bed, smoothing the cover, and rapidly tidying the locker-top, which was strewn with junk of all kinds.

'Here,' she said, finding a comb and handing it to Margaret. 'Comb your hair. It looks awful.'

'I did it half an hour ago,' protested Margaret.

'It doesn't look it. And you need some lipstick. Where is it? Here. Put some on. There, that's better.' She hurried off again to the laughter of the visitors.

'I don't know why this sudden interest in my appearance at this hour of the morning . . .' began Margaret, and then broke off with a gasp. In the reflector she saw coming towards her, walking slowly and with difficulty but on his own two feet, a tall young man with a ragged, untidy mop of dark hair. He held on to the bedhead unsteadily, looking down at her.

'Your hair!' she exclaimed. 'It's terrible.'

'Never mind about my hair,' said John Lester firmly. 'It's you I've come to see.'

The crowd around the bed had tactfully melted away, and all the other people in the ward were suddenly very busy with their own affairs. When the two young people had returned to earth from realms uncharted, Margaret asked in wonder, 'But I still don't understand. This morning I had your letter saying they were just going to let you sit up, and that you would be in hospital for a few more weeks anyway. How did you do it? Do they know you are here?'

John grinned. 'They know all right. I had the devil's own job to get out of the place. As soon as I found I could move about, I shot through.'

'Straight from hospital!'

'Sure. I wanted to see you.'

'But how do you feel?'

'Fine,' he said, looking, and feeling, as if he would faint at any minute.

Margaret decided to take the bull by the horns. 'What are we going to do about the future?' she asked. 'I don't know how I'm going to manage.'

'Not now,' he said. His face was white with the strain of having his body in an upright position. He thought it was possible he might be sick.

For the rest of the week he continued to visit her, but always he sidestepped any open discussion of whether their future paths lay together or in different directions.

Dr Cheshire soon noticed the darkening rings under Margaret's eyes, and asked her outright how she was getting on with her young man.

'I can't stand it,' said Margaret. 'I just don't know whether we're engaged or unengaged. John doesn't seem to want to discuss it.'

'I think you'd better send him to me,' said the doctor. 'I'd like a word with him, in any case.'

In his office he gave the young man a clear and concise picture of Margaret's condition. 'She will never walk on her feet again, she will always be susceptible to skin breakdown due to pressure, and to serious bladder infections. These are the bane of every paraplegic—they can lead to disaster or even death; only with scrupulous, unremitting care can they be avoided. We think we can teach some limited control of bodily functions. We may also teach her to stand in calipers, but she will probably have to rely on a wheelchair for locomotion, since her lesion is too high to permit her to walk with crutches and calipers. This is the difficult side. Now, on the positive side, there are plenty of things people can do from a wheelchair. I personally know women who run their own homes, and some who go out to jobs. It can be done with courage and ingenuity. Motherhood is also possible in many cases.'

'In Margaret's case?'

'I would say so.'

There was a silence. Dr Cheshire leaned forward, and said with great intensity, 'Look, if you are going to break off your engagement, for God's sake go in there and do it *now*, not in six months' time.'

'What I can't understand,' said John, 'is how we are going to cope with the problems of day-to-day living.'

'Then I suggest you stay around and observe the rehabilitation training given by our staff here. You'll be able to see for yourself just how people *can* cope, and cope well, with life in a wheelchair. But you haven't answered my question.'

'What question?'

'The question as to whether or not you still contemplate marriage. I have a right to ask you because Margaret is my patient, and her well-being is my concern.'

John stared at the doctor in great surprise. 'But it's never occurred to me that we'd do anything else except go straight on with our plans. Of course we're going to get married! I'm merely trying to find out how on earth we're going to manage all the practical side of things.'

Dr Cheshire sat back with a great sigh of relief. In spite of all his years of experience he had never quite mastered the art of detachment.

'Why not go in and reassure the girl?' he suggested gently.

'If you think she needs it,' said John, still surprised.

'I haven't got a shirt ironed for tomorrow,' announced Ian on his way to the bathroom late that night.

'Anyone who wants a clean shirt has to iron it himself,' declared Gerta. They had just returned from the hospital and she was exhausted.

'How was she tonight?' asked John Watkins. He was still recovering from his recent illness.

Ian paused thoughtfully over the clean clothes basket. 'She's quite different.'

'Different in what way?' asked Gerta sharply.

'Well, all this time she's been cheerful enough, but sort of quiet. Tonight she was sparkling just like she used to—it's all come back. She was simply glowing.'

'Thank heaven for that,' said her father.

The patients in the acute ward were a motley collection of both sexes, of differing ages, and from all walks of life. Many of the men were there as the result of car accidents. Adrian Black, a father of six, had fractured his neck in a diving accident. Alan Yeomans, a jockey, had suffered injuries in a pile-up of horses on the race track. There was a truck-driver, there were university students, there was a housewife.

Into this company one day was admitted a young schoolboy. Paraplegic as a result of cancer, he had been brought into the Spinal Centre so that he would not have to be in a ward for the old and the dying. For, no matter how severe the disabilities in Ward Seven, there was an atmosphere of hope and encouragement, a feeling of life beginning to flow forwards again instead of slowly ebbing away. And there was laughter.

55

So Bruce was brought in and put in the bed opposite Margaret. Every day his mother and her sister came to comfort him. Although his condition was rapidly deteriorating, the mother refused to give up hope, and kept a cheerful face. Gerta, secure in the knowledge that Margaret was alive and would soon be well, was deeply moved. The three women often talked together, and from her mother Margaret learnt Bruce's story.

As a robust twelve-year-old, avidly keen on sport, he had one day complained of a mild pain in his side. This was the beginning. An operation was necessary, and after it for a while he attended school normally. Then the cancer recurred, affecting his legs so that he was put into a wheelchair. But he refused to stay in it. He taught himself to walk again, and once more recovered to the extent of being able to go back to school. He was then a pupil of Geelong Grammar School, due for the wonderful year at Timbertop, the mountain annexe where the boys learnt bushcraft. Bruce was not well enough to cope with such activities. He remained at the main school in Geelong; bitterly disappointed though he was, he made no fuss. After that he went rapidly down-hill, and soon there was nothing for it but hospital again. Once or twice, in spite of his desperate condition, his mother had him taken home on an operation stretcher trolley in an ambulance. He had two wonderful weekends in the garden at home, shooting at the magnolia buds with his airgun, his beloved dog Timmy panting on another trolley, level with his face.

'I wish I knew what was the matter with me,' he said wistfully one night to his aunt, while his mother was out of the ward for a few minutes.

She turned away, fumbling in his bedside drawer for something to talk about. She found a pair of small keys.

'Look what I've found,' she said brightly. 'Whatever are these for?'

'Don't you know?' replied Bruce. 'They're for the trick handcuffs I got last Christmas. Tell you what, you handcuff nurse to the bed!'

The next day he died.

It was a distressing and deeply moving experience for everyone in the ward.

Only later did Margaret, thinking about it all, realize that not once had any of them heard Bruce whimper or complain.

Meanwhile, Gerta and John were realizing that not only the victim of a disaster but those close to him as well must adjust to the new situation, for inevitably their attitudes must deeply affect his own.

Impetuous and self-willed as she was by nature, Gerta felt she could never be reconciled to seeing her first-born child disabled for life. While she smiled at Margaret and talked cheerfully to the other patients in the ward, inwardly her heart ached with pity until she felt it would burst. Yet she knew instinctively that pity was not one of Margaret's needs. In her distress she found as usual that her husband's quiet strength and wisdom were equal to her need. He suggested that they should talk over their difficulties with a friend who was both a doctor and a minister of religion.

The friend told them gravely that they must learn *not to be sorry for Margaret*; that although she needed compassion and love, pity would rob her of her independence and self-confidence. She must be treated like a normal human being, no matter what happened, for only then could she function as such.

He asked them to learn this prayer, and to teach it to Margaret:

'God grant me the serenity to accept the things I cannot change, the courage to change the things I can, and the wisdom to know the difference.'

Suffering, when fully accepted, leads often to greater spiritual strength. With this attitude Gerta and John were able to set the pattern of the way in which those who loved Margaret could best help her. They gave themselves with a new maturity to the task of helping set her paralysed feet firmly on the path of rehabilitation.

five || THE NEW PATTERN
|| TAKES SHAPE

With her bed in the new position and the reflector at the right angle, Margaret took a great interest in what she could see going on in the hospital grounds. Men and women in wheelchairs scooted up and down the hill, people on wheels or on foot went in and out of the kiosk. The antics of some of the livelier spirits made her laugh. She caught snatches of conversation about basketball and table tennis—not in a wheelchair, surely!—and the possibility of getting some alcohol into the hospital (not, she gathered, for medicinal purposes).

She thought it was fun to be in a ward with men. Their robust views on life, and in one case equally robust language, added colour to her own interests. It amused them to observe her powdering her nose and trying a new hairstyle or a new tint for her fingernails. Although some had suffered far more serious injuries than she had, the atmosphere was not one either of self-pity or mutual commiseration. Everybody tried his best to keep cheerful and to encourage the one who was worse off. One man could not help groaning continuously. When the sound became unbearable Mrs Mac would yell at him, and so for a while there would be quiet. Then he would start again. When

Mrs Mac could stand it no longer she would coax a nurse to push her outside. She had recently graduated from bed to wheelchair, but she had paralysis in both arms and legs and could not wheel herself.

'I'm off and leaving yous to the blowflies!' she would shout triumphantly, as she sailed out of the ward. Her own injuries had been received in a fantastic way. On a hot summer night she was sitting with friends on the lawn, sipping cool drinks. One of the group, jumping up to fetch something, tripped and fell over her. Her neck was broken. In one unforeseeable instant she lost the power of all four limbs. She and Margaret were still the only women in the ward.

Margaret had of course been well aware for some time that she was in the acute ward of a spinal centre. She also knew that the most dangerously ill patient was allotted the position just inside the door, and was moved progressively down the ward in proportion to the recovery. She herself had held for far too long the dubious honour of being the first-bed patient; now, thankfully, she was moving down the ward. She also knew that as soon as the patients regained some degree of independence, they were taken out of the Acute Ward into Ward Seventeen, where they commenced a special programme of rehabilitation. Margaret looked forward impatiently to the time when she too would be moved there.

Nevertheless, much as she longed to 'get up and go' she still could not picture herself moving about in the world outside. 'If Douglas Bader can walk without legs, so can I, and I will too,' she said to herself determinedly—but as yet she had no idea how it could be done. Looking around at the motionless bodies, she experienced a moment of brief panic. 'Supposing a fire broke out in the ward,' she thought. 'Not one of us could do a thing to save ourselves!' The fear remained at the back of her mind—full realization had come to her that no matter how she learnt to manage her unresponsive body, in certain situations she would be helpless.

'How can I learn to be completely independent?' she asked Dr Cheshire fretfully one day when he was on his rounds.

'We're teaching you as fast as we can, my dear,' he said. 'Keep doing your exercises, and soon we'll get you out of bed and into

59

a wheelchair. When you graduate to Ward Seventeen you'll start an intensive programme of rehabilitation.'

'Yes, I know,' she said. 'But there are all sorts of things that are worrying me, like bathing and toileting and so on. I don't want to have people heaving me around as though I were a baby.'

'Don't worry. We don't want that either. And it won't be like that, I promise you.' He thought for a moment. 'I think I know someone who can help you. Just be patient for a day or two, will you, till I see if I can arrange it.'

Margaret was too much like her mother to be patient when she had an idea in her mind. She thought of his words continually, wondering if he had forgotten his suggestion. She should have known better. A week or so later a young woman in a wheelchair rolled up to the bedside and introduced herself. She was a small person with a round and happy face, and wore attractive, well-cut clothes.

'I'm Helen Gillies. Dr Cheshire says you are bursting to be independent, and he's given me strict orders to teach you everything I know about life in a wheelchair. Successful, too, I mean,' she laughed. 'Although I say it myself.'

Margaret beamed. 'It's awfully good of you to come and give time to a complete stranger.'

'Oh, you aren't a stranger to me! I know all about you. Your fiancé's cousin was one of my student nurses at the Alfred Hospital. And I've got friends in East Kew who are neighbours of your grandparents—I met them the other night when they were visiting.'

'You mean Grandad and Nonnie Watkins? They're in a terrible state about me.'

'Yes, they were,' admitted Helen. 'They belong to the generation when a paraplegic stayed in bed and was brought little posies of flowers and nourishing soups—and eventually developed bedsores and bladder infections, and died in a couple of years. You and I,' she went on deliberately, 'know that this concept is as dead as the dodo. Paralysed people today can live just as long and interesting—and *useful*—lives as anyone else in the community. If they take proper care of themselves.'

Margaret's eyes sparkled. 'I wish you'd tell that to Nonnie and Grandad.'

'I don't need to, my dear. When they saw me get in and out

60

of my car by myself, and into my wheelchair by myself, and heard that I was a tutor sister at the Alfred Hospital—your grandpa's eyes came out on stalks.'

'They would,' chuckled Margaret.

'And old Mrs Watkins twittered around me like a little bird. It was a complete revelation to them.'

'They'll be much happier now,' said Margaret. 'Tell me, do you really do a full-time job?'

'Of course. Is that what you want to do?'

'Well, I want to take a job at some stage. And I want to finish my architecture degree. But the main problem is that John and I want to get married. And I feel we just *can't* if I have to lie around and let other people do things for me. I'd simply hate it. I've got to be independent.'

'Of course. There's no reason why you shouldn't be. What you should try and do later on is get a car; you can get special hand controls fitted. Once you learn to get yourself in and out of the car and into the wheelchair you are completely free. You can go anywhere you like. It's a wonderful feeling to be mobile again.'

'I'll bet!' said Margaret fervently. 'But what about things like bathing and toileting? How on earth do you cope?'

'Look,' said Helen. 'I'll teach you every single thing I know. It's a promise. We'll start with the things you could do in hospital. Later on they'll let you go home occasionally for a weekend to get used to life outside the hospital. Then I'll come out to your home and teach you how to manage things there. We'll start today with bladder control. Elimination of body wastes is one of the chief problems a paraplegic has to deal with; compared with that the wheelchair is nothing. You *can* help yourself a lot—with training. There are a number of points that are helpful.

'Take bladder control for instance. Now, a newborn baby has no control over his bladder—if he did, half the washing-machine factories in the country would go out of business. When his bladder is full it empties itself involuntarily. It's only later when nerve connections are made that voluntary control can be established. Many paraplegics can, with training, develop the same type of automatic bladder as the baby has, and it is possible to gauge the voiding time by observing the usual interval which elapses between drinking liquids and voiding. You can also help establish regularity by stimulating the muscles at the right time, lightly tapping the lower abdomen, for instance. Paraplegics who don't have automatic bladders have to deal with the problem in other ways—and it's easier for men than for women.'

She went on explaining, clearly and concisely, step by step, what could be achieved, and how it could be done. Margaret listened eagerly. Now at last she had a guide, a girl near her own age with the same needs and problems. But as she listened she realized that her visitor was also a first-class teacher. This was not surprising for it was something of an honour to be a tutor sister at the Alfred Hospital. The Alfred, as it was familiarly called, had been founded nearly a century ago. Situated in the Melbourne suburb of Prahran, it had rapidly developed into one of Australia's most important teaching hospitals. It was affiliated with the University of Melbourne; later it was to be affiliated with the newer Monash University. It was one of the first hospitals to use a kidney machine and other modern equipment. Although it was a general hospital, patients came to it from all over the southern hemisphere for open-heart operations. The nursing, as could be expected, was of a high standard, and a nurse who was trained at the Alfred Hospital never found any difficulty in obtaining a position overseas.

Helen Gillies had just commenced work there as an attractive young staff nurse when, in March 1954, she was thrown out of a car in an accident, with the result that her spinal cord was injured, leaving her paralysed from the chest down. She was nursed with devoted care at her own hospital, but when she was well enough to move about in a wheelchair she found herself faced with many problems of daily living. These she solved the hard way, one by one, experimenting with each until she found the best way to manage. Having proved to herself that she could cope alone, she took an overseas trip to make quite sure, and then returned to the hospital to become a tutor sister, two years after the accident. She subsequently took the Diploma of Nursing Education. She had nursed paraplegic patients, she was a paraplegic herself, and fully understood the problems of being confined to a wheelchair. But they were problems that could be overcome, she assured her listener, and they need not debar one from leading an active and useful life.

'That's what Dr Cheshire's been telling me for weeks!' exclaimed

Margaret. 'And he's not the sort of person to lead people up the garden path.'

'No, he's not,' agreed Helen. 'He's completely realistic, and he usually speaks his mind. What he says, he means, you can depend on that. He's completely dedicated to his work, and he knows there's just no room for sloppy sentimentality in dealing with disabled people.'

Margaret nodded. The realistic approach was natural to her too.

'It isn't that I didn't believe him—I knew he was right. It's just that I couldn't visualize all the practical details,' she explained.

'Ah,' said Helen, 'but that's probably because you want to run before you can walk.'

The funny side of this struck them both simultaneously and they burst out laughing.

Margaret's spirits soared. Given time, she felt, nothing would be impossible.

The usual fearsome-looking gift to paraplegics in the acute ward was a pair of steel coil-springs with hand grips. Sometimes these were fastened to the bed-frame and the patient was instructed to pull on them a certain number of times every half-hour to develop strength in the arms. Margaret's were not. She used them by lying on her back and pulling her arms apart as hard as she could. This was to strengthen her arms, which would soon have to take over the tremendous task of managing her powerless trunk and legs. No matter how many of the men scamped this exercise—and many of them did—Margaret never missed, although sometimes it seemed that the entire day was taken up with physiotherapy exercises, feeding and toilet routines. She believed in her ignorance that things would be slightly easier when she was mobile. How wrong she was could be judged by the expression on Allan Abbott's face when he heard her remark to that effect. Allan was a university student whose neck had been broken in the car accident which had killed both his parents. He had graduated from bed to wheelchair with fantastic speed, and he recounted with relish the details of the famous programme which Dr Cheshire had laid down for unsuspecting paraplegics once they graduated from Acute Ward Seven to Rehabilitation Ward Seventeen.

'Compared with the Programme,' he said, 'a full day's work in the outside community is a rest cure. You will be expected to get up, get yourself out of bed, dressed, toileted and fed, all without any assistance; then you go up to the gym for an hour's exercising, under the eye of Mr Luke; when he's exhausted you you trundle down to Occupational Therapy for an hour's instruction in A.D.L.—that means Activities of Daily Living, as in a wheelchair—back to the ward for lunch; back to gym for exercising; back to O.T. for more instruction in A.D.L. In case you are bored, you then wheel yourself out into the pure, fresh air for an hour's sport: archery or basketball or whatever other strenuous form of self-torture you fancy; then you trundle yourself back to the ward for the evening meal. Your arms will be dropping off with fatigue by this time, but woe betide you if Dr Cheshire catches you letting anyone push your wheelchair. *And the rest of the day is your own!'*

'Don't worry,' said Jenny, who had just entered the ward for Margaret's daily exercises. She pulled the screens around Margaret's bed. 'You'll enjoy it, because you'll be learning how to be independent. Let's see your arm exercises. . . . That's very good. Now we're going to turn you over on to your tummy.'

Margaret was terrified. It was the first time she had been face down since the accident, and when Jenny and her assistant flipped her over she felt sure she would suffocate. They let her get accustomed to the new position, before Jenny said firmly, 'Now let me see you try some push-ups. But of course you can! You'll be surprised at the strength in your arms.'

'It's not that,' protested Margaret heatedly. 'It's—well, dash it all, I've got no clothes on, and my bed's right next to the window!'

Sister Gillings, when Jenny appealed to her, shook her head. 'If Dr Cheshire wanted Margaret to wear something on her shoulders he would have said so. Oh, I see. Well, if you can find a cardigan, you can slip it over her shoulders. But just for the duration of the push-ups. And no buttons. There must be no buttons. We can't risk pressure.'

Margaret exploded when the conversation was reported to her. But Dr Cheshire's orders, as interpreted by Sister, were as the laws of the Medes and Persians. The cardigan went on buttonless, draped and fastened somehow around her shoulders, and was whisked off as soon as the new exercises were over. They now became part of the daily routine, and very soon Margaret was

64

promised that if she continued to improve she would be able to try sitting on the edge of the bed, not an easy thing to do when three-quarters of the body was without feeling or power. Then she would be allowed to sit in a wheelchair, and gradually learn to wheel herself about. When she had achieved this she would be transferred to the Rehabilitation Ward to begin the rigorous training programme.

Gerta and Natalie were elated, and Natalie began at once to make a dressing-gown ready for the great day when Margaret would be permitted to wear clothes. She had been completely nude for nearly three months. They were all deeply interested in fashions, and now the conversation around the bedside turned to styles and colours. Of course when Margaret put on clothes again they must be as attractive as possible. A friend was already making her some new slacks. They decided she must have a lovely new pleated skirt and tights. Shoes were a difficulty. There were several dainty high heeled pairs that Margaret had collected for her trousseau, but they would be most unsuitable for a wheelchair.

'Better let me take them back,' suggested Gerta. 'The store will credit them.'

'All right, but I'm jolly well going to have pretty ones even if they haven't got high heels,' declared Margaret, who had a feminine adoration for attractive footwear. 'And Mum, Dr Cheshire says I've got to pay all my own bills and manage all my own business affairs, so please give me all the accounts.'

'Very well, dear,' said her mother, with such unaccustomed meekness that Natalie and Margaret winked at each other.

'Won't it be wonderful to be up and dressed, and outside again,' sighed Margaret happily.

But she was to learn, like every other paraplegic, that time and again when life was going smoothly the body would suddenly rebel and present its owner with the most formidable problems.

Gerta and Natalie had brought the new clothes one evening, and they were being admired by several visitors. But Margaret felt a strange lack of interest. Something queer was going on inside her. She was suddenly afraid that she might vomit. She could hardly wait for everyone to go away. Alone at last, she closed her eyes. They felt swollen and unreal, and her head was throbbing. Strange new sensations caused her to shudder uncontrollably. She felt herself sinking into black, swirling mud that would suck her down, down, to be lost forever. She called out frantically. Hands came out of the darkness, voices murmured together, a thermometer was pushed under her tongue, someone was feeling her forehead. She heard Sister Gillings's voice: '. . . infection . . . get Doctor to have a look at her . . .'

The day set for her sitting out of bed came and went. Gerta appeared mistily at her bedside and vanished again. It was night and then day and then night again, peopled with ghastly spectres.

'This is death,' she thought. 'I'm dying and nobody can save me.' She called out weakly. 'Hold my hand,' she gasped to Sister O'Dwyer. 'Don't let me die. I don't want to die.'

'You aren't going to die, Margaret. Try to rest. You'll feel better in the morning.'

Margaret clung frantically to the smooth, cool fingers. Presently the drugs they had given her began to work. She fell into restless sleep, but still she would not let go of Sister's hand.

Gradually the infection cleared up, but it left her pale and shaken. She did not know that not many years ago it was accepted that thousands of spinal cases would die each year from such illnesses. Thanks to skilled nursing, modern drugs, and the methods of rehabilitation developed by a certain Dr Guttmann, she had every chance of a normal lifespan. But these considerations were far from her mind as she lay weakly in her usual attitude, side, back, side, and now front, according to the routine of the turning team. Sitting up no longer seemed possible, or, for a while, even desirable.

Even in Melbourne with its cold and dreary winter, there are some enthusiasts who have to have their pre-breakfast swim all the year round. As was usual at this time of year the newspapers were featuring pictures of robust men and women diving into icy water while the rest of the shivering population hunted out a few extra layers of winter woollies to see them through the day.

'Why so quiet, Margaret?' asked Jenny, who was putting her through her passive exercises.

'I was just remembering how wonderful it was to dive into cool water and streak away into the distance. We've always been a sporting family—surfing and swimming are top favourites.' She spoke without self-pity, as one remembering another era.

'You're getting towards the last bed in the ward now, which

means you'll soon be up and about—then you'll be able to do some sport again.'

'In a *wheelchair*? Look, people keep telling me about this, but I can't quite see how it's done.'

'You'll see all right when the teams all gather here for the first Australian Paraplegic Games. Some of the events are being held here at the Austin. And a team will be chosen to compete in the International Stoke Mandeville Games in Rome, which follow the Olympic Games. Dr Cheshire is going in charge of them, I think, and Mr Johnston from the Perth Paraplegic Unit.'

'But why are they called Stoke Mandeville Games, if they're being held in Rome?' asked Margaret, reasonably enough.

Jenny reflected for a moment. 'The idea of sports for the paralysed started nearly twenty years ago at Stoke Mandeville, which is the National Spinal Injuries Centre in England.'

'Was it Dr Guttmann's idea?'

'Yes. Apparently some of the patients found a ball and started tossing it to each other in the ward. The sister was rather surprised when instead of reprimanding them Dr Guttmann gave them a bigger one. Then he and his staff started experimenting and found that there were all kinds of sports that could be done in a wheelchair. Basketball—'

'Basketball!'

'—skittles, snooker, archery. . . . It had such a tremendous effect on the patients' well-being and morale that Stoke Mandeville started having annual sports days. The idea caught on, and paralysed people in other centres began to play sport too. Dr Guttmann started inviting teams from overseas, and now the International Stoke Mandeville Games for the Paralysed are becoming world famous, like the Olympics—in fact they're being held in Rome after the Olympics this year. You can imagine the marvellous effect all this has on people who still have the old idea that paralysed people can't do anything except sit in a corner or lie in a bed till they die.' She glanced at Margaret's face, but there was no response. It is one thing to hear something with one's ears; it is another to accept it. Margaret had had no experience of wheelchair athletics, and simply could not visualize anything of the kind.

She was still unconvinced when within a week or so the Austin began to buzz and hum with an influx of disabled people. High-spirited men and women raced about the grounds in their wheelchairs; the terrain was neither smooth nor level, but the visitors' daredevil antics on their back wheels kept the spinal patients constantly amused as they watched eagerly in their reflector mirrors. Some of the people came into the ward, bringing excitement with the latest reports of their doings. Interstate competition was keen. Victoria had its own first-class athletes. Three of the Austin's own patients, aboriginal Kevin Coombs, Bruno Moretti, and Fred Martin, were strongly tipped to be chosen to represent Australia at the Rome Games.

But if Margaret was slow to see the possibilities of paraplegic sports, Gerta was not. She missed no detail of what was going on. She saw the wheelchair table-tennis tournaments in the hospital's Zeltner Hall, thinking to herself, 'Margaret could do this.' She and John Watkins went off to Albert Park to watch the field events, and she came back to the ward full of enthusiasm.

'I wouldn't have believed it!' she said. 'Margaret, they race around in their chairs just like able-bodied people. There was one girl from Sydney, Charlene Meade, a little older than you. I saw her at the table-tennis, and today we saw her doing archery. That's something you could do, too.'

'Archery!' exclaimed Margaret. 'Heavens, you have to sit upright and hold your bow and arm absolutely taut—how could I do that?'

'You might learn. Anyway, another thing, Charlene is married and has a two-and-a-half-year-old daughter. She runs her own home from her wheelchair.'

'Does she! I'd like to meet her.'

As it happened, Dr Cheshire, who never lost an opportunity to help his patients, had already asked Charlene to visit the ward. She wheeled herself in a day or two later, a smiling, curly-haired, firm-featured young woman in a blue track suit.

'Of course you can have a happy marriage even if you are disabled,' she said. 'It means that things are slightly more difficult, and everything you do takes a little longer than it does when you are on two legs, that's all. As a matter of fact, my husband is disabled too, but he has a good job. I run our home and we have a beautiful daughter. And I'd like to have a son. When you are ready to be married, if you can manage a trip to Sydney, come and see me. I'll show you everything I do, if it's any help.'

68

'It would be wonderful. I could stay with Auntie Joan. John and I hope to get married in November, so I guess it would be about October if I came.'

'October of this year!'

'Well, I want to get going. I'm tired of hospital.'

'Naturally,' Charlene laughed. 'Just write and let me know.'

'I will. Thank you very much. It will be terrific.'

The exhaustion left by the bladder infection had now vanished, and Margaret found herself once more eager to try sitting up. At last the day came. Natalie's new gown was pulled around her bare body, the physiotherapist Jenny Sanders, together with the Sister, swung her gently round until she was across the bed, her legs dangling over one side. Gently they raised her body to a sitting position.

'You can support yourself by pressing on the palms of your hands,' directed Jenny. 'How does it feel?'

'Absolutely weird. Now I understand the term disembodied spirit,' murmured Margaret, fighting dizziness and nausea.

'Could you try removing your hands?'

She did and immediately toppled sideways. The two women expertly caught her and set her straight again.

'You see,' explained Jenny, 'there is a kind of muscular memory which helps us balance our bodies. As a baby you learnt to sit up and balance, but you can no longer do this in the same way because of the paralysis, so you have to learn to do it all over again. You have to depend more on your eyes at first. Take a bearing in regard to what you see around you, and try to keep yourself upright. Watching yourself in a mirror helps, too. We'll practise that way later on. Had enough now?'

Margaret nodded faintly, on the edge of unconsciousness.

'It's always like this the first time,' comforted Jenny as they eased her back to her customary horizontal position. 'It will be easier each time.'

The sitting was rehearsed daily, until one morning Jenny appeared propelling a wheelchair, followed by two other physiotherapists.

'Am I going to gym today?' asked Margaret excitedly.

'Steady on, eager beaver! You've got to get used to the chair first.'

They fastened the dressing-gown around her, and sat her on the edge of the bed.

'Make sure the chair is braked,' said Jenny, rapidly lacing Margaret's shoes. 'Yes, you have to wear these, in case your feet get knocked. Mustn't risk a skin-break.'

Working as a team, the three of them lifted her bodily and deposited her, no featherweight, in the chair.

'There. How does that feel?' asked Jenny, tucking a sheet around Margaret's legs.

'Awful. Like sitting on a floppy old aircushion,' she gasped, flopping about like a carelessly stuffed rag doll, and holding grimly on to the armrests. 'I don't seem to be sitting on *anything*. And I'm going to be sick, I think—'

'Oh, no, you aren't.' Jenny swiftly tilted the chair backwards and held it in that position until Margaret's greenish face regained its normal colour. 'This has to be practised too, a few minutes longer every day, then half an hour daily and so on, until you can stay in it all day.'

Margaret couldn't imagine holding her balance upright for half an hour, let alone a whole day. Nevertheless she begged the team not to tell Gerta, as she was planning a surprise. The next weekend, when they knew the family would be coming, they dressed her for the first time since the accident. Tights, new skirt, sweater, shoes. They lifted her, still a floppy rag doll, into the wheelchair, and pushed her out of the ward. The lobby seemed as strange and exciting as the shores of America might have looked to Columbus and his crew. She traded the tremendous effort of keeping herself upright for the joy and excitement of the family when they walked in and discovered her. But after a few minutes the familiar nausea and giddiness returned. Answering their delighted questions with a fixed smile, she prayed silently that they would go away quickly. At last they departed. Back in the ward, after an endless afternoon, she didn't even have the satisfaction of being able to crawl on to her bed and collapse. She had to wait for the staff to put her back to bed. It took another week or two before she could remain in the chair and wheel herself about for a length of time with any degree of comfort, and it was still always a relief to be put back to bed.

She had just reached this stage of her convalescence when one day the turning team marched purposefully into the ward and headed straight towards her. Instead of turning her they lifted her bodily and dumped her like a roly-poly pudding into the wheelchair beside the bed.

'What on earth—?' she gasped, as the nurse began to clear her locker, while the three men grabbed all her possessions and began stuffing them into pillowslips.

'You're moving off. You're leaving us!' He plonked a bulging pillowcase on to her lap and stood there rubbing his hands and grinning. 'Anything else, nurse?'

Before she knew what was happening she was whisked out of the ward, along a path, up in a lift and into a small bedroom. The two beds were made up and empty. The team piled hers with the bulging pillowslips and all the junk from the top of her locker, and rapidly disappeared. She heard the nurse telling someone that Margaret Watkins had arrived, she heard a faint reply and then complete silence. The silence seemed to go on for hours. Nobody came near her. It was the first time she had been alone for over three months. After a long time she realized that no one was going to help her sort out her belongings. This was the beginning of the new regime. Independence. She began slowly, with infinite awkwardness, to put away her own possessions.

Some memory stirred dimly at the back of her mind. What was it . . . ? She groped for it several times in the weeks that followed. Then one day it returned to her in a flash. The transfer from the tender care of the Acute Ward to the robust atmosphere of the Rehabilitation Ward made her feel exactly as she had felt when she left Junior School and started the year as a new and rather apprehensive member of the Senior School.

six || REHABILITATION WARD

Nearly one hundred years ago a cook by the name of Louisa developed tuberculosis while working in Victoria for a family of graziers, the Austins. Mrs Austin treasured her cook very dearly, and was distressed to find that Louisa, being a household servant, would have to go into a prison hospital for treatment. For some time the Church of England in Melbourne had been agitating for a place for the treatment of incurable diseases. Mrs Austin took up the cause and in 1882 helped found the Austin Hospital for Incurables. It had sixty-six beds, and the cook Louisa was one of the first occupants.

Thereafter it rapidly developed into a general hospital, with a T.B. ward for children, and spinal, chest, orthopaedic and cancer units. It was only a matter of time before it was to become a teaching hospital, and in 1966 an appeal was launched for funds to erect a new modern hospital with every possible facility.

The Spinal Injuries Centre was conceived in 1956 by the late Dr Tom Patrick, then Medical Superintendent. With the active help of Dr Donald Duffy, Dr Keith Bradley and Dr John Cloke, it was developed by the Austin Hospital and the Hospitals and Charities Commission of Victoria into a comprehensive centre for the treatment and rehabilitation of patients with spinal-cord injuries. The only other fully developed spinal centre in Australia at that time was at the Shenton Park Annexe of the Royal Perth Hospital in Western Australia, directed by Dr George Bedbrook. But the Australian public was beginning to hear of the success of these two units in treating spinal patients who were formerly considered hopeless. Also, Dr Ludwig Guttmann, Director of the famous Spinal Injuries Centre at Stoke Mandeville in England, in personal visits to Australia, gave unlimited advice and encouragement. Soon other Australian States were beginning to think of having their own spinal centres.

To begin with, Margaret knew little about paraplegia and less about rehabilitation methods. But with her natural curiosity and her obstinate determination always to know *why* she was expected to undergo a certain treatment or practise a certain exercise, she soon pieced the story together.

It was not so many years ago, she now knew, that paraplegics were regarded as chronic incurables, and were put aside to die, which they usually did in two or three years, mostly as a result of pressure sores and kidney infections. But there had been a dramatic change in all this.

When the Second World War broke out, the civilian and military medical authorities in Britain realized that a large number of young servicemen would inevitably become paralysed as a result of war wounds, and at last active steps were taken to try to reduce the appalling mortality of this condition. There were few doctors who had much experience of the problem. Spurred by the great need, the British authorities under the Churchill government took the imaginative and probably unprecedented course of appointing to this vital job of treating British and Allied servicemen a man who was an enemy alien. This man, who was to chart new pathways in medical science, was Dr Ludwig Guttmann. Dr Guttmann had been the Neurosurgeon and Director of the Jewish Hospital at Breslau, in the German province of Silesia, until the rising tide of Nazi persecution compelled him and his family to seek refuge in England. He had first encountered the problems of paraplegia in his early impressionable years as a doctor when he was treating injured coalminers in his native Silesia. Even then he had been certain that better results could and should be achieved.

Now, in 1943, he had his chance to tackle what was to him an absorbing problem of medical research and at the same time to express his gratitude to his adopted country. He was given accommodation, at first only one ward, in a new Emergency Medical Services hospital at Stoke Mandeville, near Aylesbury, in Buckinghamshire. Within a few years he had revolutionized the whole approach to the problem, his teaching had spread new hope to disabled people throughout the world, and the National Spinal Injuries Centre at Stoke Mandeville had become a world-famous institution with over two hundred beds. Eventually he was to be knighted for his work.

Guttmann's methods, Margaret was told, included acceptance of the disability, intense development of what muscle-power remained, occupational therapy, and re-training for the patient's old job or, if necessary, preparation for a new one. Scrupulous care must be taken of the paralysed body to prevent the dreaded skin-breaks and infections. He made people realize, at last, that it was not the spinal injury by itself that made people sick or killed them, but the avoidable complications of being paralysed. So if he and his team could become good enough, then, with the right training, a paraplegic could look forward to a normal life-span and, indeed, a normal life in the community. To add weight to this, Guttmann conceived the idea of paraplegic sports. A man feels just as good as the next one when he is part of a team striving together for a first-class performance. Moreover, the general community can see this with their own eyes, and they develop a new and healthier attitude towards disabled people. Starting in a simple way with men and women in wheelchairs throwing balls or darts, Dr Guttmann and his staff soon began to organize sports days. Each year saw new developments in the field of paraplegic sport. Before long teams were visiting Stoke Mandeville, first from other districts in England and then from overseas, until eventually the doctor conceived a more daring idea. He suggested that every fourth year the International Stoke Mandeville Games should be held in the city of the Olympic Games, immediately after these Games had concluded. This great step forward was first made in 1960, when the Games were held in Rome. On that memorable occasion, 425 athletes from 23 nations competed. This international sports movement has continued to develop; and community understanding of the conquest of paraplegia is due in no small measure to the development of paraplegic sport.

Knowledge, training and experience so often count for nothing and go to waste where there is no motivation to use them. There is something deeply stirring about a doctor's desire to devote his entire life to people formerly considered hopeless cases. The young Jewish doctor's fierce compassion for his paralysed coal-miners kindled a spark that flamed into action to help thousands of suffering people. The same compassion motivated other medical men baffled by the problems of paraplegia. One of them was a young Englishman by the name of Cheshire.

David Cheshire was a young orthopaedic registrar when he met his first paraplegic patient. To his dismay he found he virtually did not know how to treat her, nor were his textbooks any help. He watched her slowly succumbing to all the worst complications of paralysis, which would inevitably lead to her death. After several weeks during which her condition rapidly deteriorated, it was decided to call Dr Guttmann into consultation, as by now, in 1949, Guttmann's reputation and his work at Stoke Mandeville were beginning to be known.

Dr Guttmann was a short, stocky man, with keen eyes behind his rimless glasses. His expression as he looked down at the unfortunate patient was printed on the inexperienced young doctor's mind for all time. If the senior man did not actually use the words 'grossly incompetent treatment' it was probably because he was restraining himself from some stronger expression.

'Is there any possibility at all of saving her?' asked young Cheshire.

The man who had been forced to flee from his own country because he had the wrong ancestors looked straight at the young Englishman.

'Not only will we save her,' he said abruptly,' but we will restore her to a useful life in the community.'

It was no coincidence that Dr Cheshire was later to be found at Stoke Mandeville, and that his life's work was to be the treatment and rehabilitation of paraplegics.

Early in 1959 he arrived in Australia to become the first full-time Director of the Austin Hospital's Spinal Injuries Centre, and within a short time the influence of his vital and positive approach made itself felt throughout the unit.

Margaret's admission was well-timed—it was at the beginning of the following year that she became a patient in the Centre's Acute Ward.

After three months in the Acute Ward with only a sheet for covering, it seemed queer to be wearing clothes again. In bed Margaret now wore a nightie—Natalie had made a bright red one to celebrate the occasion. It had a slit up the back because it was important not to lie on any folds of material which might redden the skin. In Ward Seventeen Margaret found she was expected to toilet and dress herself with as little assistance as possible. She needed no urging. The first shower was a red-letter event. She inspected the recess eagerly. There was a smooth, scrubbed wooden seat attached to the wall, and enough room to wheel a chair alongside; by taking out the side of the chair she could slide awkwardly on to the shower seat. Terrified as she was of slipping, she was nevertheless elated to find that the taps were within reach. She could actually shower all by herself. On the first occasion the nurse hovered nearby; after that, Margaret coped on her own. Once she had transferred herself back to the wheelchair, she could dry and dress herself, slow and tedious though this was at first.

The nursing staff in Ward Seventeen were just as careful of the welfare of their patients as were those in the Acute Ward. But since their charges were usually up and about in their wheelchairs, they did not see quite so much of them. One of Margaret's favourites was Sister Wilson. A motherly and understanding person, her mere presence was often a comfort to those patients who while putting on a good front, were deeply troubled about the future. But all those who made up the team, be they doctors, sisters, nurses, therapists or makers of crutches and calipers, had one united aim, which was to rehabilitate their patients and send them back into the community able to take care of themselves.

The day was now all mapped out with gymnasium work and occupational therapy, with every activity designed to train the disabled patient to manage himself. For Margaret this spelt marriage to John; with this goal in mind she set off eagerly for

76

her first session in the gymnasium. The women usually trained in the gymnasium in the '3KZ' Block, which was named after the Melbourne radio station whose listeners had provided the funds to build it. There Elspeth and an assistant worked with the patients, with Mr Luke, the senior physiotherapist, visiting often to inspect and advise. Several patients were already at work when Margaret first arrived. Some were weight-lifting, some practising standing in calipers, and some exercising on mats.

Margaret's first tasks in the gymnasium were to improve and perfect her balance. This she did by watching herself in a mirror and by performing other balance exercises. Then, as her balance improved, she was able to progress to the more difficult tasks of rehabilitation. Weight-lifting and hauling on pulleys with weights attached were performed over and over again. This was a favourite opportunity for gossiping as the women sat in their chairs pulling away and chattering to pass the time.

'I want you to do some mat work now, Margaret,' said Elspeth one day. 'You get down by controlled falling,' she went on, reading Margaret's thoughts as she looked nervously at the floor, a long way below her wheelchair. 'Lean forward—careful not to over-balance too soon—pull up your footplates, take hold of your feet and place them on the floor; now fall out! Careful not to knock any skin off.' This last was an automatic refrain to almost every instruction given to a paraplegic.

Margaret followed the instructions and, to her surprise, found herself lying on the mat, none the worse for her fall. Here she was taught how to manoeuvre and manage her paralysed body. It was not, she found, an entirely useless body, as her unfeeling legs could be used as a support for sitting or kneeling. She diligently practised bending, toe-touching, and push-ups. The latter were particularly important, as paraplegics were instructed to lift their bodies often from their chairs to prevent pressure sores. To get back into her chair she was told to face the chair in a kneeling position with footplates up, place her hands on the arm-rests and lift herself into the seat. Try as she would, she never was able to achieve this, although she saw many other people succeed. Her lesion was too high, and she was not a light-weight. She found it a severe blow to her pride that she always had to be helped back into her chair.

There was a bed in the gym with overhead ropes and pulleys.

Here she practised transferring from bed to wheelchair and vice versa, also turning and moving in general, again to prevent the dreaded pressure sores and generally promote good health. She was also taught to dress and undress herself, and she practised eagerly, trying to do it more quickly at each attempt.

It was pleasant being able to talk freely with women again. In Ward Seventeen men and women had separate quarters, meeting together for all meals except breakfast. They ate at tables— another step back to ordinary life—on an open verandah. Some of the boys were very high-spirited; occasionally Margaret would retire to a closed-in area and eat with a dear old man who looked like a koala bear, and who told her about his grandchildren.

'And how are you getting on, my dear?' he would ask her.

'Very well, thank you. It's wonderful to be up and about.'

With her rapid progress in the gymnasium she was beginning at last to feel that independence was on the horizon.

'When will I be able to go home?' she asked Sister one day when she was having help in putting on her socks, a chore she had not yet quite mastered. But Sister was not listening. She was frowning over one of Margaret's feet.

'How long have you had that skin-break on your foot? You are supposed to examine yourself every day with a mirror and report any skin-breaks at once.'

'What skin-break?'

Sister showed her a patch as large as a coin on one heel.

'You'll have to go to bed, Margaret. Get undressed and doctor will come and see you. He'll probably keep you there for a week at least. Perhaps two. These breaks on the extremities are difficult to heal because circulation isn't good in those regions.'

Margaret was furious. Just as she was beginning to make some progress in her rehabilitation programme she was put back to bed, forbidden to have showers. Her wheelchair was taken away and she was placed in a carefully designed position that would allow no pressure on the offending foot. The worst part however was the humiliation of having her visitors see her in bed again. She had been so proud of being up and dressed. She gritted her teeth, read innumerable books and counted the days until she could start her programme again. The time seemed endless. Her room-mate, Mrs Viney, comforted her.

'You're young, dear. That's all in your favour.' Mrs Viney was a middle-aged Tasmanian, who on an afternoon's outing to watch a football match, had been struck and made paraplegic by a falling goal-post. In spite of the difference in their ages she and Margaret were good friends, each trying to comfort and encourage the other. Mrs Viney was just as delighted as Margaret when the foot was finally pronounced healed and Margaret was allowed to resume the daily programme. Her boisterous companions on the verandah welcomed her back heartily; but she had not long been up and about when another move was announced. All women patients were to be transferred from Ward Seventeen to Ward Eighteen, on the floor above.

Ward Eighteen contained mainly women and quadriplegic men, so that the atmosphere was on the whole quieter than in rumbustious number Seventeen. The sister in charge, Sister Plant, was a young married woman with light-brown hair and a pleasant manner. She had been introduced to Margaret some weeks previously when she was making the ward round with Dr Cheshire to meet the patients who would shortly be under her care. Sister Plant took a great interest in the personal problems of her patients, and privately worried about the ones who were neglected by family and friends during the long months in hospital. It was so important for those long-term patients to keep their morale high. Margaret she regarded with great satisfaction, for John Lester's attentions and the devotion of the Watkins family and friends provided sufficient incentive for Margaret to throw herself whole-heartedly into all the activities of rehabilitation.

Margaret was quite content with the change, except that she found that architecturally the showers and toilets were not so easy to manage as they were in Ward Seventeen. She usually had to ask a nurse for help, which she felt was a blot on her precious independence. There was one terrible occasion when the nurse went away and forgot her, naked, wet and shaking, awkwardly balanced on the shower seat, unable to move because her wheelchair had been left just out of reach. There was no one within call. She simply had to remain there until someone found her by chance, a long time later.

The quadriplegics, or quads, as they were called, were those whose spinal injuries were so high that they were partially or completely paralysed in all four limbs. It might have been expected that around these men would be an atmosphere of hopelessness and sadness. On the contrary, terrible though their predicament was, from the verandah where they foregathered repeatedly came the sound of lively speech and spirited argument. This was largely due to the influence of a big man called Ken Slater, to whose side patients, staff and visitors gravitated as to a magnet.

Ken Slater had a brilliant scholastic and sporting record. At Camberwell Grammar his achievements had included being dux and Captain of the school, Vice Captain of football, Captain of tennis, and the honour of scoring three centuries at cricket. He had taken a science course at Melbourne University, had taught at his old school, then held various positions in the sporting-goods trade. He was a successful management consultant when he was injured as the result of doing a good turn: he had been driving some friends to their destination when the car accident occurred. Completely paralysed except for his head, he devoted his waking hours to the welfare of disabled people. Among other things he had helped establish a hostel for them, and he had assisted substantially in the organization of Australia's first paraplegic games. In the Spinal Centre he made it his business to encourage patients whose disabilities were in many cases less severe than his own.

'All right, so you can't use your body. But your brain isn't paralysed, is it?' he would say to any patient who might be temporarily depressed at his own condition.

To show what could be done he founded the Paraplegics' Debating Society, which subsequently won the B Grade Championship of Victoria; he then proceeded to coach them to A Grade level.

If everybody loved Ken, the younger boys openly hero-worshipped him. Among the latter was a teenager by the name of Bill Mooney. Bill had been an apprentice engineering draughts-man, a keen footballer and swimmer, until the day he dived into a country swimming pool and broke his neck on a submerged tank. Helpless from the neck down at the age of fifteen, and desperately ill over and over again with the recurring infections common to his condition, all he wanted to do was die. Life for him, he thought sullenly, was over before it had even begun; it might as well end completely now. While Dr Cheshire and his staff set to work to make him change his mind, it was Ken who

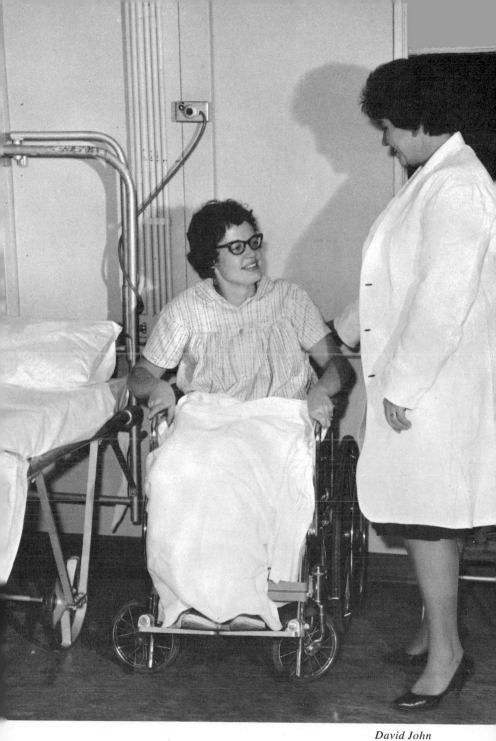

David John

Acute Ward: learning to sit in a wheelchair for the first time, helped by physiotherapist Jenny Sanders

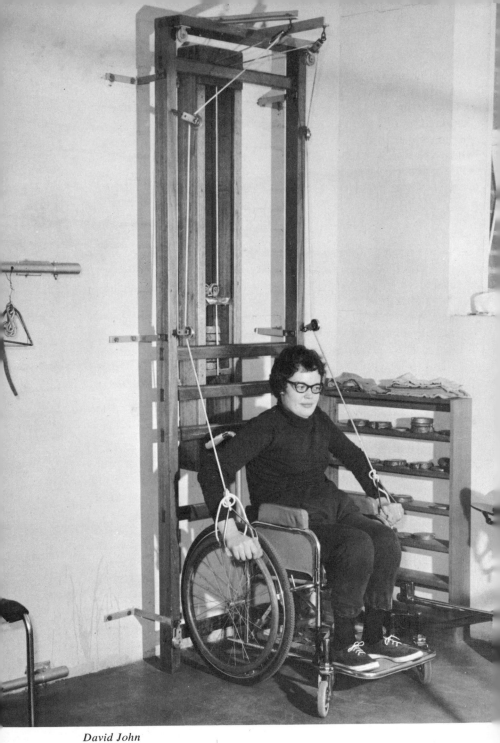

David John

In the gymnasium: pulling on weights to develop arm muscles

quietly saw to it that the boy's bed and wheelchair were always next to his own, and it was Ken who argued, cajoled and bullied him into the realization that the riches of the mind need not be despoiled by the plundering of the body. From there, Ann Pennington, the Senior Occupational Therapist, took over. The therapists never ceased to plan and carry out endless ways in which their most helpless patients could regain some degree of activity and independence. Ann had pondered over Bill Mooney's difficulties for a long time, and finally had come up with a suggestion that was to bear more fruit than either of them suspected.

Observing the struggles of many quads to rehabilitate themselves, Margaret reflected soberly that she had indeed been fortunate that her own injuries were less severe than theirs. She shuddered to think that had her spinal injury been only an inch or two higher she too would have been completely helpless. But she was learning through experience that though the body may be bound, the mind can be free, and the spirit—limitless.

Rolling her chair into the occupational therapy department one day after a busy session in the gym, she found Bill Mooney sitting in his chair with an easel rigged up in front of him. A bottle of brushes and several small pots of paint were nearby. Coming closer she saw there was a fine pen drawing pinned to the easel. It was a lithograph of an old Melbourne building.

'Hullo, what's all this?' she asked. 'Don't tell me you are colouring that lithograph!'

'Why not?' he grinned. 'Watch this.' Completely helpless from the neck down, he seized a brush with his mouth and dipped it steadily into the blue paint. With delicate strokes he tinted the background of the lithograph.

'Marvellous!' exclaimed Margaret. 'Heavens, I couldn't do as well with my hands.'

'It was Miss Pennington's idea. She dreamed it up a few months ago,' he said shyly. His face was shining with the tremendous pride of having discovered something he could *do*. 'I didn't realize I was artistic till I tried. Miss Pennington's combed Melbourne for every lithograph she can find.'

Margaret found that Bill practised his new art nearly all day long. In fact he amassed such a pile of exquisitely tinted lithographs that Ann Pennington decided she would arrange an exhibition. Moreover she was going to ask Lady Paton, wife of the Vice Chancellor of Melbourne University, if she would open it. Lady Paton was a woman who herself had had a great deal of personal experience with physical disability. As it happened she knew Margaret quite well through her own daughters who had attended the same school; she had been a visitor to the Acute Ward in the early difficult days when Margaret's jaws had been wired together. She now characteristically took the trouble to visit the Austin again so that she could make Bill Mooney's acquaintance before the exhibition.

The lithographs fascinated her. 'They are beautifully done,' she said warmly, 'and no doubt some people will want to buy them. They are well worth it. But what are you going to do next?'

'I hadn't really thought,' answered Bill.

'Well, you see,' said Lady Paton, 'there's only a limited market for this sort of thing, so that if you want to be independent by selling your work, it seems to me you need to be thinking of some other kind of painting. Why don't you paint that girl?' She indicated Margaret, who was sitting nearby, in her wheel-chair. 'Or those hills that you can see out there?'

'I'd never thought of it,' said Bill. 'I don't know whether I could.'

'Couldn't you try? How about giving him a blank sheet of paper next time, Miss Pennington?'

'I will,' smiled Ann. 'And, Lady Paton, when you open the exhibition the patients would like to present you with something made in the occupational therapy department. Is there anything you'd particularly like to have?'

'Well now,' said their visitor graciously, 'I've always wanted a really nice laundry basket.'

'Margaret, you can make that for Lady Paton,' said Ann as she conducted her guest out of the room.

'Golly!' exclaimed Margaret when they were out of earshot. 'I've never done any basket-work in my life!'

Bill wasn't listening. A young man whose arms, legs, and trunk were powerless and unfeeling, he was turning over and over in his mind the incredible words 'independent by selling your work'.

As it happened, Lady Paton's words were to come true. A number of artists became interested in Bill Mooney, among them an armless painter, Athol Thompson of Ferntree Gully, who was

82

a member of Rehandar, the abbreviated name for Reproductions of Handicapped Artists, which was the Australian branch of the International Association of Mouth and Foot Painting Artists. Bill's teachers launched him into an intensive course of painting. He made such good progress that with Athol Thompson's help he eventually became a member of Rehandar himself. Full membership meant regular work and a guaranteed income. A new life opened out for Bill. He showed his appreciation in turn by passing on his own skills to two more Austin quadriplegics, Roland Marks and Bruce Peardon, who also were eventually admitted to Rehandar.

Ken Slater died in 1963 as a result of his injuries. He had known that his days were numbered, and he had spent the last months in drawing up a questionnaire on the possibilities of employing handicapped people in industry. He personally delivered a brilliant paper on the subject to the Institute of Personnel Management only four days before the end. He had lingered long enough to see Bill established in an absorbingly creative career, although he did not see the sequel—Bill as a happily married man living in his own attractive home in a suburb of Melbourne. He himself had been denied the chance to marry and have a family of his own. But there are children of the spirit even as there are those of the flesh. To the sullen and desperate child in the bed beside him Ken Slater had surely passed on the gift of life.

Bill was not the only patient to rejoice in the activities initiated by the occupational therapy staff. O.T., as it was familiarly called, was to Margaret a picnic after the rigorous demands of physio-therapy. Gerta had seen to it that all her girls were accomplished in the housewifely arts of cooking, sewing and laundering. Now all Margaret had to do was adapt her skills to the limitations of a wheelchair, and the O.T. staff gave her every opportunity of doing so.

In the new ward she had for the first time a room-mate of her own age, a New Zealand girl called Dawn. They found rehabili-tation more interesting when they did things together. In the ward they were taught together how to get themselves in and out of the bath. They raced their wheelchairs to and from '3KZ', they practised cooking, learned to do their laundry and ironing from their wheelchairs.

When Dr Cheshire cunningly showed Margaret a picture of the wedding of paraplegic Susan Sinclair, a Stoke Mandeville 'Old Girl', to Lord Masham, the pattern of her own future began to crystallize further in her mind. She could see herself running a home for John and caring for his needs just like any other wife. She redoubled her efforts towards rehabilitation. Soon, she thought hopefully, she would be completely independent. And then, as usual, her rosy plans were again brought to a standstill.

Ward Eighteen was on the second floor. To go to the occupational therapy hut the girls used the lift. The lift buttons were at the right height for their wheelchairs and it gave them a wonderful feeling of power and satisfaction to control the motion with their fingertips. But the way to the gymnasium was down a long ramp from the second storey to the ground, along the roadway and over a little bridge. This was the girls' favourite speedway. They were tearing along it one day when Margaret's chair struck a pothole just outside the gymnasium and overturned. She was thrown out violently on to the ground.

'Are you all right? What shall we do?' asked Dawn, whitefaced.

'Find someone to lift me up, I suppose.' Margaret propped herself up on one elbow, feeling both foolish and angry. It was so humiliating to be completely helpless on such an occasion. She couldn't even wriggle out of the way if a car approached too fast to see her. She raged inwardly while Dawn fetched some men to lift her back into her chair. And of course the worst had happened. Her knee was bruised and swollen, and the skin was broken. It only needed one glance for Sister to send for the doctor, who naturally ordered complete bed rest. Margaret was compelled to obey. Back she went to bed, and there she had to remain until her leg was completely healed, which took some weeks. When she eventually resumed work in the gymnasium she gritted her teeth and practised over and over again the drill for getting herself off the floor into her wheelchair. It was still absolutely beyond her strength. 'But I'll do it some day. I will. *I will*,' she vowed silently.

The occupational therapy staff were constantly devising new ideas to stimulate and encourage their patients. Their latest idea was that Margaret and Dawn should give a dinner party. They must plan the menu all by themselves, order their stores, cook the meal in the O.T. kitchen and serve it to the guests of their choice.

'We must ask Dr Cheshire,' said Margaret.

'And Sister Plant.'

'And Jean Murray.'

'And Ann Pennington.'

'And Fay Odgers.'

'That'll be seven, counting ourselves. I guess that'll be enough people. What shall we give them?'

'Apple strudel!'

'Yes, with lots of cream.'

'What about steak and kidney pudding?'

'Soup to start with!'

'And coffee to end with!'

They had a wonderful day. Two wheelchairs simultaneously busy in one tiny kitchen did not leave much room, and there were one or two minor collisions and a near-spill. But at the appointed time all was ready: the bench beautifully set, flowers arranged, and tantalizing smells floating out to greet the guests on their arrival. It was a gay, happy party. Sister Plant kept them in fits of laughter with her stories of the pranks in her ward.

'The other night,' she said, 'a possum fell down behind the ward wall and made such a frightful noise that no one could sleep. The boys sent for the night orderly, and, brave man, he got the poor creature out from behind the panel by dazzling it with his torch.'

'How on earth did he get it out of the ward?' inquired someone. 'Did he chase it out?'

'No,' said Sister Plant. 'He tied the belt of his gown around its neck and led it away to the gardens! It was a sight I should like to have seen. The boys related the whole story to me next morning, very vividly. Quite the highlight of their week!'

They all laughed, sipping their coffee contentedly after their delicious meal. Every one of them had totally forgotten that the two hostesses were in wheelchairs.

seven || PREPARING TO RE-ENTER THE OUTSIDE WORLD

Margaret had seen various paraplegic patients wearing calipers to practise standing and walking. She knew that her own turn would come as soon as she had done enough strengthening exercises to prepare her arms and shoulders to take the extra weight that they would have to support. For as well as her paralysed trunk and legs, the calipers themselves were heavy. Specially designed for each patient, their purpose was to form rigid splints for the legs so that the patient could learn to maintain an upright position.

The more a patient stood, the less he would be likely to develop pressure areas from sitting too much. Also, the upright position was good for the general circulation of the blood and the health of the internal organs. Margaret knew all this and was eager to co-operate. She observed with interest the process of being measured and fitted for her own calipers. But when the leather and iron braces actually arrived and were fitted on her in the ward, her heart sank. They were so very heavy and cumbersome; and, something that irritated her feminine instinct, the shoes she had to wear with them were the plain-Jane, sensible, flat-heeled lace-ups worn by every school-girl.

'We'll try standing now,' said Mr Luke, when Mr Masson, the splint-maker, had satisfied himself that the calipers were a good fit. He wheeled forward a rectangular walking frame with two front wheels. 'You can hold on to this.'

The two men assisted her to an upright position and let her maintain it alone, holding tightly to the frame.

'How does that feel?'

It was dizzying yet exhilarating. 'It's marvellous! I'd no idea I was so tall!'

'You are too tall for this frame. We'll have to order one specially for your size. Now we'll show you how to take off your calipers. From now on, every time you go to the gym take them with you, and when you've done your other exercises, put them on and the physios will show you how to get ready for ambulation.'

'But that means walking!'

'That's right.'

'Impossible,' said Margaret to herself; and, as it happened, she was very nearly right, for in this aspect of rehabilitation she met her Waterloo. Getting the calipers on to her legs—and after the first time she had to do it always without help—took half an hour at least. It was a terrible struggle. There was a further struggle to pull herself upright. Sometimes the physiotherapist assisted her with a push on her backside, which helped jerk her up. She would maintain this position by clinging desperately to two horizontal parallel bars. As soon as she had developed confidence the two leg braces were strapped together and she was shown how to move forward. This was achieved by bearing down on the rails with all the strength of her arms, hands and shoulders, and at the same time lifting her heavy lower body up and jerking it forwards. Repeated many times, it gave her a slow forward progress which was termed ambulation. This achieved, she was shown how to balance out of the parallel bars by leaning on elbow crutches. To her dismay she found she was expected to ambulate with these. She co-operated, as usual, to the best of her ability; she was always more than willing to practise wholeheartedly anything that would help her achieve independence. But this last activity was almost impossible. She simply could not visualize herself doing the simplest of household tasks while trying to balance on crutches. When she found herself required to learn how to get up and down kerbs and steps she outwardly followed

87

instructions; privately she had already made up her mind that walking was not worth it for her. She would re-organize her life from her wheelchair.

She almost changed her mind however when she came into 3KZ one day and found that her own specially ordered walking frame had arrived. With the calipers on and legs locked together, it was possible by pushing it to move forward in a series of bunny-hops.

'This is rather fun,' she said. 'I think I'll use it to hop back to the ward.'

'But you can't do that!' said the physiotherapist. 'It's miles away, and right through the parking area. The ground's very rough in some places. Oh, very well then,' she laughed, as Margaret was already half-way out of the gymnasium. She dialled the ward number and spoke to Sister Plant. 'Would you mind keeping Margaret's lunch hot, please—she's walking back to the ward.'

The phone crackled with astonishment.

'No—her walking frame has arrived, that's all. Oh, and if she doesn't turn up at all you'd better let us know!'

The antics of wheelchair athletes as seen in her reflector, and the stories they had brought into the Acute Ward, had made wheelchair sport seem very exciting. Seen in retrospect they made Margaret's own initial participation very tame indeed. Sport then was largely controlled by the occupational therapy staff. They had worked out a cheerful programme for the women, which involved sitting on the verandah and throwing darts to strengthen their arm muscles. Margaret, at that time the youngest of the group, was listed with the dart players; she hated darts, and went reluctantly to her verandah while the men raced off to wheelchair basketball, a noisy and vigorous outdoor game.

'Why can't I play basketball?' she asked.

'Too rough, Margaret. It's a man's game.'

'But I don't like darts.'

'Never mind. It's good for your arm and shoulder muscles.'

Margaret's chance came when Dawn became her room-mate. Together they badgered the staff until they were given permission to play with the men. The staff were quite right; it was a rough and somewhat risky game, but it was tremendous fun and very stimulating.

There was an archery range outside the Occupational Therapy Department. The other women patients were not very enthusiastic about archery, nor was Margaret herself particularly drawn towards it, but with her determination to try out her own powers she decided she would give it a chance. She found, as she had feared, that the effort of sitting upright, and holding bow and arm taut, was almost beyond someone who had no control over her torso. It was no help to be informed that that was precisely why it was prescribed. Some years later a wheelchair friend told her of a specially reinforced corset which could be worn to keep the body under control. For the present, Margaret thankfully exchanged her bows and arrows for table-tennis bat and balls, which she found much easier to manage. John Watkins had long ago built his own table for the family—they all played well—and she found it was really not so much more difficult from a sitting position.

The sport that she was most anxious to try out was swimming.

'I want to find out what happens when I get into the water,' she said to Jan Emmett, one of the occupational therapists.

'Have you always been a good swimmer, Margaret?'

'Well, my sister Natalie is really the family swimming champ. But all of us live in the water in the holidays, and in term time we used to get up early to train in the Camberwell baths. If I could just float or paddle about it would be something, wouldn't it? Do you think I'd be able to?'

'We can't tell until you try,' said Jan thoughtfully, 'and there's no swimming pool here. If we could find some pool where you could try yourself out I'm sure I could get permission to take you there. One of the men patients has been asking too. We'd need a physio to help get you in and out of the pool.'

'What about the Beaurepaire Sports Centre at the University? I've often swum there after lectures, and I know the man in charge, Bill Tickner. I could ring him.'

'What's it like for access?'

'There are stairs. But they do have glass doors that slide back to get equipment in, and they are level with the parking ground —I guess we could be classified as equipment!'

Mr Tickner was delighted to classify two Austin paraplegic patients as equipment.

'That's just fine,' he said. 'Come on up any time—just let us know when to expect you.'

Within a few days the Austin party arrived by car at the Beaurepaire pool: Margaret and her fellow paraplegic, escorted by Jan Emmett and a tall, curly-haired physiotherapist called Harrow Morgan who had promised to lift the patients in and out of the water.

But once in her swimsuit and sitting precariously on the edge of the pool, Margaret suddenly became overwhelmed with nervousness. Supposing she sank to the bottom and drowned! Her hands clung desperately to the edge; balancing upright was still a tremendous effort.

'I'm ready,' she said quickly, not giving herself the opportunity to change her mind. She felt herself being pushed forward. The warm water enveloped her, down went her head and legs, up came her rear, she began to choke and splutter, completely out of control and terrified.

'Try on your back,' came Jan's composed voice.

She felt herself being expertly flipped over; the air rushed into her lungs. She was breathing.

'You're afloat,' said Jan.

Margaret lay in the water while her panic subsided. After a few moments she made some cautious arm movements under the water. 'I'm moving! I'm moving!' she called excitedly.

'Yes, you are! Slowly but surely. Now turn over on your tummy again and try hanging on to the side.'

But once again Margaret lost control and was completely terrified. She screamed for help. Jan flipped her over on to her back. Feeling safe once again she resumed her careful arm movements. Before long she was swimming slowly up and down the pool on her back. It was marvellous. When the time came to return to the hospital it was all they could do to coax her out of the water. 'I'm swimming!' she kept saying incredulously. 'I'm swimming!'

Margaret was beginning to feel that she had reached a new stage in her rehabilitation. Her slow recovery in the Acute Ward lay behind her like a bad dream. The early difficulties and achieve-

90

ments of the rehabilitation training programme had turned into acts which were now merely tedious repetitions. She wanted to leave hospital.

Dr Cheshire was cautious. 'We don't like to let patients go unless we are quite sure they can cope with the outside world,' he said. 'What would be your immediate plans?'

'I'd like to go to Sydney and stay with my aunt so that I could visit Charlene Meade and see how she runs her home and family in a wheelchair. Then I'll come back and get married myself.'

'You need to take it gradually. I suggest you begin going out for an occasional excursion. Get John to take you. You can also start going home for weekends as soon as your family can convince us that the house is livable for a wheelchair person. Would you like to come with my wife and me to an exhibition tennis match tonight?'

'Thank you. I would.'

Margaret reported this conversation to the family, and astonished some friends by saying that she'd like to be taken for a drive on her first outing: they had thought the accident might have left her nervous. The only nervousness Margaret felt about cars, however, was how she was going to get in and out of one under Dr Cheshire's eyes when he took her to the tennis match. Mr Luke had recently shown her the way a paraplegic could manage this. Margaret felt a little like a schoolgirl asked to play her examination piece to the headmistress. She fled to the men's gymnasium and obtained Mr Luke's permission to practise in the physiotherapists' carpark. When it was time to leave for the tennis match she slid from her wheelchair into the Cheshires' car with all the nonchalance she could muster, and the doctor watched with approval.

Meanwhile, John Watkins was considering her access to the family home. The house had a big old-style verandah reached by several stone steps. John decided to by-pass these. He designed a long wooden ramp with exactly the right gradient, and such pleasing proportions that when the men of the family had finished erecting it, it made quite a graceful addition to the house. At the same time Gerta was collecting pillows for a soft pressure-free bed. Fortunately the family toilet and bathroom were suitable without any modification. As soon as the ramp was ready they brought their daughter home for an experimental weekend visit. They stood aside to let her wheel herself up the ramp and into the house. As they saw her delight, and the rapturous welcome of her brothers and sisters, perhaps their greatest emotion was of gratitude that her life had been spared. In spite of minor difficulties the weekend was a great success.

The next venture was a visit to the theatre with John Lester. There was a railway station a stone's throw from the hospital, so the two of them rode in the guard's van all the way to the city to see the opera *Porgy and Bess*. Margaret had not known the story of the opera. It was a poignant experience for her to watch the hero being jeered at because he was a cripple. She and John decided that they detested the term 'crippled'. They thought it was too often associated with pity, and charity, and hand-outs. Disabled was a much healthier word.

Once she had begun going out into the community again Margaret's old zest for life was a thousand times strengthened. She could hardly bear to miss anything she heard about, whatever it might be—concert, film, party or exhibition. Whenever she was able to obtain leave from the hospital, John willingly escorted her, although neither of them had much money and they had to do things as simply as possible. They also had to save for the future. When they were not exploring the sounds and sights of Melbourne he visited her in the ward. But unrestricted visiting only applied to the Acute Ward. Now Margaret could only receive visitors in the evening. In any case, John often couldn't get to the Austin until fairly late, which did not please the Sister at all. She took Margaret to task for too many outings and too many late nights.

'But that's what I'm being rehabilitated *for*,' expostulated her patient, who thought that her activities should be regarded as proof of the success of the Spinal Centre's methods.

But Sister, whose concern was that her patients should have enough rest and sleep, did not agree.

A few days later Dr Cheshire, in making his rounds, was addressed by Margaret, waiting in her wheelchair.

'I want to ask you about my discharge from hospital,' she said.

'Yes, of course. We decided you'd probably be ready in about three weeks' time, didn't we?' They had had many discussions on the subject.

'Could I go sooner?'

92

Dr Cheshire hesitated. 'When?' he asked cautiously.

'Now, please.'

He showed his astonishment. 'Well! Isn't this rather sudden?'

'Not really. After all, I've been in hospital seven months.'

'That's actually a very short time indeed for a patient with a high spinal lesion. The majority take eight or nine months. Some take even longer if there are complications, or if the home background is unsuitable.'

'But I've got a job, and it starts on Monday,' she informed him casually.

'A job! What job?'

'At the Ideal Homes Exhibition. For three weeks. The Timber Development Association wants an architecture student to demonstrate and explain the features of their exhibit. So I applied. And got the job, subject to your approval, of course. Dad says he'll take me in every morning, and John's father will bring me home.'

Dr Cheshire, long accustomed to the heartbreaking struggles many paraplegics had in making the transition from hospital back to community, said feebly—for him—'Do you think you will be able to manage all right?'

'Well, of course. Why not?'

He looked at her quizzically before he replied, 'In that case I suppose we'd better see if we can arrange to let you go!'

'Don't forget,' said Dr Cheshire when she eventually wished him goodbye and thanked him for all he had done, 'always come back to us for check-ups, and for any help you need at any time.'

'I will.'

Brimming with enthusiasm for the future, she wheeled herself happily out into the sunshine where Gerta was waiting. Grateful for all the Spinal Centre had given her, she was too modest to realize how much she had unconsciously given in return. Many a patient, secretly despairing over his plight, had been encouraged by Margaret's cheerful determination to overcome all the difficulties of paraplegia. Her positive, matter-of-fact approach, her continuing zest for life, and her refusal to brood over what couldn't be helped, inspired all who came in contact with her. Now that she was to rejoin the community outside, more people were to be encouraged by her unconscious example.

eight || ARCHITECTURAL BARRIERS MAKE BACK-DOOR CITIZENS

Margaret had left the Austin Spinal Centre with the determination that no physical disability was going to stand in the way of her leading an active, normal life. She had reckoned without one factor: The community she lived in did not take the disabled into account when designing its houses, its streets, its public facilities. She was to have a slow and by no means pleasant awakening.

It began with church. The religious life of the family had always been centred in the local church, which they attended regularly. The children went to Sunday school, sang in the choir, and took part in many fellowship activities. John Watkins was a member of the Vestry. Sometimes one of the family read the lesson. In hospital Margaret had taken Communion during special bedside services. It was natural that on her return home one of her first outings should be to St Mark's for Communion Service. She would have liked to wheel herself in quietly and resume her usual participation in the service with the rest of the family. But steps to every entrance made that impossible. Ian had to lift her chair into the building. Once inside, steps to the altar prevented her from wheeling forward to the Communion rail. She had to wait until the sacred bread and wine were carried down to her, as they were carried to the parishioners from Broughton Hall, an establishment for elderly people, many of whom attended St Mark's and sat in the front row.

'For years I've looked at those people and felt sorry for them, and now I'm one of them,' thought Margaret. For the first time it was forcibly brought home to her that old age as well as accident brings its disabilities. Sitting in her chair, ranked with those people whose physical strength was not enough to take them to God's table, she thought of the way her religion, as long as she could remember, had given her comfort and a sense of purpose in life. How many disabled people, she wondered, stayed away from church because they couldn't manage wheelchairs, or crutches, or calipers up and down steps leading into a building? Margaret was lucky to have young men in her family who were able to help if they were with her. Moreover, on her next visit to church Mr Gair, one of the churchwardens, came hurrying to meet her, his face wreathed in smiles as he showed her a small ramp that had been specially made for her and any other wheelchair members of the congregation. It was to be kept inside the vestry door and brought out whenever they saw her coming.

But people were not always so considerate. Mentally she reviewed the various churches and cathedrals she had visited over the years. Her trained inner eye visualized high stairways, narrow aisles, awkward doorways. What about people with heart conditions? And the very old, or the blind, who found stairs so difficult without a handrail to grip or guide? From churches her mind leapt to a dozen other buildings. Colleges and schools, banks, post offices, insurance offices, places of entertainment. How could a disabled person transact his daily affairs if at every turn he was blocked by stones and bricks and wood which made unnecessary barriers for the wheelchair, or for the faltering feet? How extensive were these barriers, and need they exist at all? Couldn't buildings and roadways be designed for the use of both disabled and able-bodied people—for the same cost, and without detracting from their good appearance? She resolved to find out for herself.

'There is some grave injustice here,' she thought, looking at the people beside her, and slipping compassionately into prayer as the service began.

Her chance came a few days later. Everyone else had gone to work or school except Gerta, who on doctor's orders was resting in bed. Margaret brought her a tempting breakfast tray, straightened the covers and kissed her.

'I'm going off shopping for my trousseau,' she said gaily.

'Are you, darling? Wouldn't you like to wait till I feel better?'

'No. I'd like to try all on my own. It'll be fun bowling down Burke Road to the Junction. I'll be all right. Now, don't you do anything silly while I'm away. Expect me when you see me. I'll bring back something nice for your lunch.'

'How about crossing the roads, darling?'

'Well, I've seen the boys at the hospital go up or down a step in their wheelchairs,' hesitated Margaret.

'So have I.' Gerta sat up suddenly. 'They give their chair a violent jerk back on their two back wheels so that they are suspended in mid-air at an angle of forty-five degrees, and they jerk forward and crash down again on to the step—one inch more and they'd fall on their backs and crack their skulls! Don't try that, for goodness' sake.'

'All right, Mum. Don't spill your coffee. I wouldn't be game, so don't worry. If the pavement hasn't a ramp into the gutter I'll just wait until someone comes along to help. Goodbye for now.'

She shot off down the long ramp at the side of the house and out into the street. Down their own driveway, across the road, up an opposite driveway, and then along the Ryeburne Avenue pavement towards Burke Road, one of Melbourne's busiest arterial roads. She had never even noticed that it was a hill, in the days when she used to hare along on her two feet to catch the Burke Road tram. Now, on her first journey alone in the wheelchair she felt nervous and uncertain. She steered herself around the corner into Burke Road and found a driveway into the gutter with another opposite. Waiting until there was a lull in the traffic she shot across the busy highway, terrified of being hit by a speeding car. Turning the chair she was now facing her destination, the shopping centre at Camberwell Junction, where six main roads formed an intersection; but outside St Mark's she had to halt at the traffic lights. There was a drop into the gutter, impossible for her. Cars and lorries whizzed past. She waited.

A woman with a pram and three children milled around and passed her as the light turned green. A pause while the lights turned red. An old lady waiting to cross looked at her with sympathy.

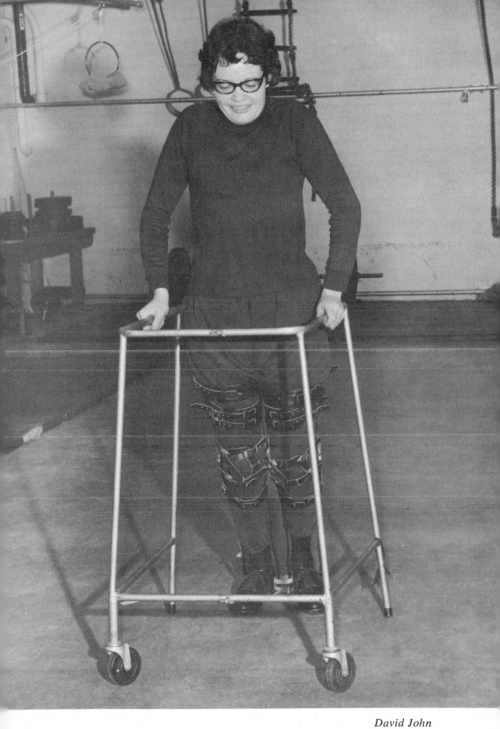

David John

Wearing calipers and learning to walk with a walking frame

Herald-Sun, Melbourne

John and Margaret Lester, 19th November 1960

'How long will you be in the wheelchair, dear?'

Margaret, who loathed sympathy, gritted her teeth and smiled brightly. 'All my life.'

'Tut-tut! It's wonderful that you can be so cheerful!'

The lights changed and the old lady pattered across.

A middle-aged woman with a shopping jeep and two baskets rushed forward to catch the green light. Margaret let her go. The lights changed again several times before she found her mark, a worried-looking matron with a large basket and a bulging handbag.

'Would you mind pushing me across the street, please? I can't get the chair over the kerbs.'

'Of course, dear. Should you be out on your own?'

'I'm quite all right. It's just that I can't manage the kerbs.'

The lights changed again while the woman loaded Margaret with her own basket and handbag. She charged across the road with the wheelchair, nearly tipping her passenger out, and struggled to get it up the opposite kerb.

'You have to tip me back, first. Farther back. I won't fall out.'

She thanked her helper, returned the basket and bag, and set off alone to bowl herself down to the Junction. But the smooth, easy run she'd been anticipating turned out to be a myth. The pavement, like so many others, had a definite slope towards the gutter. This meant that the balance of the chair had to be maintained by a tremendous effort of her right hand. Very soon her arm was aching furiously, but she dared not relax lest the chair run down into the gutter.

Nevertheless, it was fun to be out alone, in spite of the stares, to which she had not yet become accustomed. There were no less than five side streets to be crossed on her way to the main shopping centre. Each meant a pair of kerbs impossible for her to manage. She simply had to sit and wait patiently until someone passed by who could be asked to help.

'Just as well it isn't pouring with rain,' she thought resignedly, again trying to ignore the curious stares. She was not going to let them spoil her outing.

She called to see her employer at Décor Gifts and thanked her once again for the mobile that had hung over her bed in the Acute Ward. She browsed happily in various shops, and bought some delightful undies for her trousseau. She found something tempting for Gerta's lunch, bought fruit and vegetables for the family. Going past a beauty salon, the familiar smells of damp hair and perfumed shampoo tempted her—she needed a haircut, anyway. In she went, her wheelchair hung like a Christmas tree with string bags and shopping baskets, her lap piled with brown-paper parcels. The girls fastened a cape over all and attended to her in her own chair.

But it had been a long and tiring morning for her first excursion alone. Burke Road looked very steep from a wheelchair when she came out of the hairdresser's shop. Her arms were still aching. She gave in and called a taxi. Hurling parcels on to the back seat with abandon, she slid herself thankfully in and let the driver pack her folded chair into the boot. It was a wicked expense, but it was worth it. *All kerbs should have ramps for prams and disabled people*, she noted carefully.

The next such expedition was to Chadstone, a large new shopping area like a miniature city, the pride of Melbourne suburbia. This was easier because John Lester had borrowed a car to go in search of a wedding suit, and she could rely on his help.

'More kerbs,' she thought as he dropped her near the shops and went to park the car. She watched the women and children threading their way between the parked cars, and waiting to cross the road. 'Some day I'll have a hand-operated car, I hope, and then there'll be the business of finding a parking spot that isn't miles away from the place I'm going to—it's not only the distance, it's all the kerbs, and the traffic that has to be dodged en route. *Parking areas should have several special places reserved for disabled people. They must be wider than the average because it's impossible to get a wheelchair between two cars parked side by side.*'

Chadstone was quite good for wheelchairs, at least with John's help. Although the inner area had two main levels, there was a lift for those who did not care to use the escalator. A few years later a ramp was to be built between the two levels. Being hauled up a flight of steps in a wheelchair was always a nightmare. The chair had to be turned around, tipped back and hauled up backwards by sheer brute strength, step by step. It was not a job for the elderly, or for a person with a bad heart. The person hauling the chair had to be very able-bodied indeed. He had to brace his feet very firmly—one slip and the chair would crash out of control, hurling out the passenger, who would no doubt be badly hurt. *Public places with flights of steps should also have graded ramps, or lifts, and the lift buttons should be within arm-reach of a seated person.*

Public telephones were another facility denied to many disabled people. The conventional red booth was quite impossible for a wheelchair. How did disabled people manage in an emergency? She had read in a publication for the disabled a suggestion that paraplegic drivers should always carry with them a sign with 'Help' written on it in illuminated red tape. This they could hang out of the car if necessary. That would work if one were on a road where there were plenty of cars. But to be in a wheelchair next to a phone box and yet be unable to use it was ludicrous. *Why couldn't there be a few open roadside telephones as there are in some places in America?*

One problem Margaret often found on her outings was getting into places where doorways were too narrow. These, and places with turnstiles, had to be by-passed altogether.

'Some shops will never know how many customers they lose,' she remarked to John. Sometimes, too, when she was shopping, she found the aisles too narrow. She would set off between two long tables of goods, and, finding herself hemmed in, would have to reverse through a crowd of irritable shoppers and their children. Once, looking for materials, she discovered too late that she was catching some of the delicate fabrics in the wheels; she could not avoid marking them with grease.

Her greatest embarrassment, however, was in connection with public toilets. She found that she shared this with many wheelchair users.

'It isn't the chair,' one fellow paraplegic had remarked bitterly. 'That's nothing. It's your own jolly bowels-and-bladder that drive you up the wall.'

Every normal adult regards these matters as his own personal concern, which he should have the right to attend to in decent privacy. In this respect many disabled people, especially women, have acute problems which the rest of the community are spared, and they must solve them, if they can, according to their own needs and capabilities; every person is different. The community is bound to provide toilet facilities wherever human beings gather for any of the activities of daily living. Why on earth, thought

99

Margaret, do they seldom if ever consider the people who often need them far more than the average? Why don't building regulations provide for this?

She had begun to go into the city for various reasons, with Gerta, and soon she knew exactly the very few rest-rooms that would accommodate a wheelchair person. Nearly all had doorways that were too narrow, turnstiles, flights of steps. One place she went to had toilet compartments just wide enough to admit the chair, but allowing no space to turn or close the door. Yet her chair had been specially made narrower than usual so that it would be easier to negotiate. She simply had to leave the door open—into a room almost lined with floor-length mirrors—while women shoppers, powdering their noses, lingered in astonishment.

'I've met paraplegics who simply never go out in public at all —now I know why,' she said grimly, when she rejoined Gerta.

Every public building should have at least one toilet compartment suitable for a wheelchair. Its minimum width should be three feet three inches, and the door should be at least two feet eight inches wide, and should open outwards.

'Heavens,' she said on one occasion when she was blocked by a turnstile. 'You'd imagine there'd be an alternative of some sort. People just don't think. One of the fellows from the Spinal Centre went to a football match the other day. They couldn't get his chair through the turnstile—he had to pull himself up on to an overhead bar and swing there like a monkey while some people folded his chair and lifted it across. It just isn't funny.'

Every sports ground or arena should have provision for disabled people.

She reaffirmed this wholeheartedly at a later date when she was competing in the Victorian Paraplegic swimming events at the famous Melbourne pool built for the Olympic Games in 1956. She found that the competitors, all disabled, and many of them in wheelchairs, had quite an obstacle race even to reach the water. First they must manage a turnstile or have a gate specially unlocked for them, next they must negotiate steps up to the concourse, then more steps to the change-room, and, of course, back to the concourse again. Most competitors had then to be lifted in and out of the water.

Some of the more daring characters slipped on to the footplates of their chairs, balanced on the edge of the pool and slid in. To get back they performed incredible manoeuvres with head and hands. It was fantastic to watch, but Margaret was too cautious to try it herself. Wheelchairs are not rounded. Concrete is hard. Modern swimsuits are skimpy. She had already too often paid the price of the thoughtless act which resulted in the dreaded skin-off. She preferred to play safe.

'A disabled person could probably get in and out of the water alone if the pool had a raised edge,' she thought. 'Something to hang on to. Or, of course, a hydraulic hoist with a seat that swings out over the water.'

With her dual special interests in rehabilitation and architecture, she continued to make, after every new experience, a careful note of ways in which buildings might be adapted so that every disabled person using them could lead a full and useful life. Very often she was appalled by her discoveries. So many places, so many avenues of employment and of entertainment were closed to the disabled, when, with just a little thought and very little money, slight modifications could make all the difference. Nearly all existing buildings needed some alteration. But if designers of new buildings could bear in mind the needs of the disabled, difficulties need not arise at all.

As time went on Margaret discovered that her voice was only one in a rising chorus of protest from all over the world. The problems of disabled people were becoming more and more acute because their numbers were growing to such vast proportions. Science has learnt to save more bodies, but very often those bodies have some disability. Science is enabling people to live longer—and there are more geriatric problems. Modern transport produces more and more accidents on the roads, particularly with the increased number of teenage drivers. More leisure brings in its victims from swimming, boating and other mishaps in the water, particularly diving. Many quadriplegics receive their injuries from diving into shallow water or from breaking their necks on a submerged obstacle. The burden of maintaining these people lies heavily on the community, but the financial loss is as nothing compared with the wastage of manpower in trades and professions. Yet these human resources are very often not used, merely because of a problem concerned with bricks and mortar—*the problem of inaccessibility*.

101

'It's incredible!' exclaimed Margaret when she heard that an intelligent fourth-year quadriplegic university student had been advised to change his entire course merely because the lectures he needed to attend were upstairs and no lifts had yet been installed.

The university was sympathetic and helpful in its attitude towards disabled students—there was no suggestion of discrimination. It was merely the old question of architectural barriers.

Once, at a university function, Margaret was sipping coffee with Lady Paton and some friends from her old school staff.

'I'll say goodbye,' she said to them. 'I go down the back way.'

Lady Paton put down her cup and saucer with alacrity. 'Actually, I'm not so keen on stairs, either. I'll come with you.'

The function was on the first floor of the Union Building. There was at that time no passenger lift, only a tiny service lift for transporting food up from the kitchens. They crammed themselves into it, almost touching the walls, and descended into the smell of boiled cabbage. One of the kitchen staff had to be asked to manoeuvre the wheelchair over a step at the side entrance; only then was Margaret able to wheel herself outside. Lady Paton confided that it was not the first time she had used the service lift. 'They're quite used to seeing me flit through the kitchen, as sometimes I bring elderly friends down this way to avoid the stairs. I always say that you can't expect old chooks to behave like spring chickens,' she chuckled, as they bid each other goodnight.

Later, a larger lift was installed. At night it was locked, but a special ramp had been built in the cafeteria entrance, and some other facilities for disabled people. But there were many places —libraries, lounges, music-rooms—where it was impossible for them to go without assistance. The toilets, too, were barely wide enough.

What was needed was a concerted attack on the problem, such as had been made in various Scandinavian countries, in England, and in the United States.

In the U.S.A. the University of Illinois had had its own Rehabilitation-Education programme for nearly twenty years. To serve disabled students, more than a hundred ramps had been built leading into university buildings, and countless other modifications had been made to even the oldest and most awkward buildings. Every new structure that was added was designed with

102

the severely physically disabled in mind. *The students were not given any form of help whatsoever.* But entrances, telephone booths, desks and beds, showers and toilets, cafeteria service, dining, library and laboratory facilities were all made equally usable by both the able-bodied and the physically disabled. In one particular year, 1959 to 1960, 181 severely and permanently disabled students attended regularly and full-time. Of these, 122 were confined to wheelchairs. Many had compound disabilities, such as the totally blind with both arms amputated, paraplegia with amputation, ambulatory paraplegia with amputation, paraplegia with epilepsy. Sixty-one of them were women, of whom forty were confined to wheelchairs.

These students lived in normal university residence halls, attended all regular classes, and took part in radio, television, musical and choral groups, fraternities, sororities, self-governing groups, wheelchair football, basketball, baseball, track and field sports, archery, swimming and square-dancing.

In 1959, at the Annual Meeting of the American President's Committee on the Employment of the Physically Disabled, individuals interested and qualified to attack the problems of architectural barriers met with key personnel from the American Standards Association. The result was the project for 'Making Buildings and Facilities Accessible and Usable to the Physically Handicapped'. It was to be co-sponsored by the President's Committee and the National Society for Crippled Children and Adults, with the latter assuming most of the financial responsibility. A large proportion of the research would be done under Professor Timothy Nugent's direction at Illinois University, where 'six disabled students had received Ph.D. degrees, twenty-two Master's degrees, one an M.D. degree, and one had become an ordained minister. Nine were on college staffs; others were in sciences, business and teaching. All were serving admirably where needed most.'[1] Almost sixty professional and trade associations, societies and government agencies also took part in the project.

After two years' intensive research the project presented a set of standards to make buildings accessible to and usable by the disabled, aged and infirm. Their specifications were approved and adopted by the American Standards Association, and immediately

1 From *Design of Buildings to Permit their Use by the Physically Handicapped*, by Timothy Nugent.

103

the sponsors began a nation-wide campaign to 'make front door citizens of the physically handicapped, and enable millions of crutch and wheelchair users and victims of heart disease and other infirmities to take part in active community life'.[2]

In Britain similar moves were taking place as a result of the growing awareness of the need to provide for the disabled in community life. The Disabled Persons Employment Act of 1948 stated that an employer of more than twenty people must have among his labour force not less than three per cent of registered disabled persons. This made it easier for physically handicapped people to obtain jobs; it also, in many cases, drew attention to the problem of architectural barriers in places where disabled people worked and lived.

Early in 1961 the director of the Polio Research Fund and the managing director of the Building Trades Exhibition discussed the matter with the officials of the Royal Institute of British Architects. They decided to promote a research project with the object of publishing a manual of technical information on architectural designing for the disabled. The project was to be financed by the National Fund for Research into Poliomyelitis (and other disabling diseases), with support from the Building Trades Exhibition Ltd. It was administered through the Architectural Association School of Architecture. Help was willingly given by many organizations in Great Britain, Canada, Denmark, France, Holland, Norway, Sweden, and America.

The resulting manual, *Designing for the Disabled*, prepared by Selwyn Goldsmith, was published in 1963, and presented a mine of information for anyone concerned with making buildings suitable for use by the disabled.

'Every individual will at some stage in life be handicapped by a temporary or permanent physical disability,' stated Selwyn Goldsmith in the introduction to his book. 'All buildings are used by disabled people, and it is the architect's responsibility to consider the requirements of the disabled people who will live, work, play or study in the buildings which he designs.'

Another committee, consisting of representatives from a wide variety of associations from councils for the disabled to the Royal Institute of British Architects, was convened by the British

[2] From 'Architectural Barriers', *Easter Seal Bulletin* (National Society for Crippled Children and Adults, U.S.A.), vol. 24, No. 8.

Standards Institution Council for Codes of Practice. Their *Draft of British Standard Code of Practice for Access to Buildings for the Disabled* was issued for comment in 1965. When the work is finalized the results will doubtless be far-reaching and beneficial to the entire community.

In Australia, interest was slowly being aroused but it had not yet gathered momentum.

'I look forward to the day in the not-too-distant future when every building and facility will be usable by everyone, the able-bodied as well as the physically handicapped,' said Leon Chatelain, Past President of the American Institute of Architects, in launching the American campaign to abolish architectural barriers; '. . . when all people can truly work, play and live together; when an individual in a wheelchair can attend the church of his choice and not be kept away because steps forbid him to enter; when he may enjoy a football or baseball game or attend a concert or the opera; when there will be no need to have specially built schools to be used only by physically handicapped children, for all of these buildings will be open to all who desire to enter. . . . Most important is the day when we can use the tremendous manpower of the rehabilitated physically handicapped that is now going to waste, for instead of being dependent on public assistance they will be gainfully employed in buildings which are freely accessible. The economic potential is enormous, but, more important, we will have people who are happy because they are at work in productive, useful occupations.

'A little co-ordinated planning can open up whole new worlds to millions of people, and all facilities will truly be open to everyone, regardless of race, creed, colour or physical handicap.

'This is the challenge and goal for all of us to achieve.'[3]

[3] From *Architectural Barriers—A Blueprint for Action*, by Leon Chatelain Jnr.

nine | MARRIAGE

'My wedding day,' said Margaret to herself for the hundredth time. It was 19th November 1960. It seemed incredible to Margaret, as it did to many other people, that it was only nine months since the day the Lesters' car had hurtled into the gully and so many happy plans for the future seemed to have been shattered. Since then Margaret had spent seven months in hospital; she had taken a job for three weeks; she had visited Sydney where Charlene Meade had shown her every detail of housekeeping from a wheelchair, and had returned to Melbourne convinced that she could cope equally well. Dressed now in skirt and sweater, she was sitting in her wheelchair dreaming, while all around her boiled the usual preparations for a large family wedding. Bridesmaids and relatives darted to and fro, people arrived with packages and telegrams, the phone rang incessantly.

'You'd better start having your bath, Marg,' said Natalie, glancing at the clock as she expertly zipped Josephine into her bridesmaid's dress.

'Yes, it's getting late.' Josephine bent down and tested her sister's bare toes. 'Your toenail polish is dry. It looks wonderful. Why didn't you let Beverley do your fingernails too?'

106

'Because painted fingernails aren't proper for a bride,' said Margaret primly.

Sixteen-year-old Phillip Watkins dashed past in his best suit. 'Aren't you going to start getting dressed, Margaret?' he called.

Ian's head, magnificently topped with a huge busby, appeared around the doorway. Drum Major of the Scotch College Pipe Band, he was gorgeously attired in a kilted uniform, staff in hand.

'Hey Marg, aren't you going to get ready?'

Margaret wished they would leave her alone. She knew exactly how long it took her to bath and dress herself, and she wasn't going to be pushed around by anyone, especially on her wedding day. She watched Natalie adjusting Josephine's hem.

'We're getting ourselves all ready so that we'll be free to help you,' said Natalie.

'I won't need any help except for my hair, and Pat Butcher's coming to do that.'

Gerta bounced into the room. 'Darling, I really think you should start having your bath now. Time's getting on.'

'In a minute.'

The family held a consultation in the kitchen.

'She won't budge!' exclaimed Natalie. 'If we don't get her started she'll have to be married in her skirt and sweater.'

'Girls are often a bit difficult on their wedding day,' Gerta reassured her. 'Don't worry—I'll get her going. Where's Ian?'

Margaret dreamed for a few minutes longer before wheeling herself in a leisurely way to the bathroom. Although elated, she felt curiously relaxed as she went through the now-familiar routines: undressing in her chair, sliding on to the toilet, back into the chair. She turned on the taps, and waited for the bath to fill. She carefully tested the temperature of the water. She lifted her feet into the bath. Then, placing a soft towel over the edge, she put one hand on the back of the bath and the other on the side; taking the full weight of her body on her hands she slid into the tub, taking care not to let any part of her paralysed body bump against taps or hot pipes. The slightest skin-break could so quickly lead to disaster.

Once in, she lay peacefully buoyed up by the water. The sounds of activity in the house were now distant and subdued; only a faint murmur of voices or the occasional slam of a door penetrated her trance-like state.

Suddenly there was an ear-splitting rattle of drums directly outside the window. Margaret pushed on the bath edge and heaved herself up in astonishment as, with tremendous power and volume, the magnificent melody of 'Scotland the Brave' vibrated through the bathroom, played, as it should be, on the bagpipes.

Margaret gave a piercing scream which brought the entire family running to the bathroom door.

'Are you all right, darling?' shouted Gerta innocently above the skirling of the pipes.

'Ian's pipe band has arrived to escort me to the church,' called Margaret distractedly, 'and I've only just got into the bath!'

'It's all right, Marg,' reassured Natalie and Josephine, who were trying not to giggle. 'They're a bit early. You've still got plenty of time.'

But five sets of bagpipes and a trio of drums could be calculated to rouse anyone to action. Margaret finished her toilet in record time, and very soon the bridesmaids had the satisfaction of seeing her sitting in her chair in the exquisite white gown designed by herself to look good in a sitting position, while friends skilfully adjusted her tiara and veil.

The music had now stopped, and the kilted musicians were forming up ready to lead the bridal procession the short distance to St Mark's. Later they would form a guard of honour and pipe the married couple from the church. A crowd of neighbours and children, attracted by the music, waited at the garden gate. Margaret smiled at them as she wheeled herself slowly down the ramp on to the garden path, her father walking proudly beside her. Natalie and Josephine and John's sister, Marion Lester, followed in gowns of buttercup yellow. As the procession moved up the street more and more children fell in behind as though Margaret were a nuptial Pied Piper. At the busy Burke Road highway car drivers gladly halted to let the procession cross to the church. Here John Watkins was permitted to push the wheel-chair, and Phillip Watkins and Natalie's friend Cliff were graciously thanked as they lifted it up the church steps.

But at the door, with John Mallinson's organ music sounding from within, and John Lester waiting at the altar, her father took the traditional place at his daughter's side. Margaret might not be able to fulfil her childish dream of walking down the aisle to join her beloved, but she had made it quite clear that if she could not take herself thither on her own two feet, she was at least determined to propel herself with her own two hands.

If it were possible to project mass emotion on a radar screen, a striking image would have appeared at that moment when John Lester rose to deliver the traditional speech. A wedding is commonly an emotional occasion; there are few people who are not touched by the sight of two young people, deeply in love, making their vows before God and society, and starting a new life together with high hopes for the future. The young see bride and groom as romance personified; older people relive their own experiences of joy and sorrow, and say a silent prayer for the couple.

But when the bride is in a wheelchair, completely paralysed from chest to toes, it is not the same at all. Those who knew Margaret and John best, and who were close to them during the period of their rehabilitation, had little doubt of their ability to build a happy and successful partnership, whatever the circumstances. But there were many people at the wedding—and it was a big wedding—who had openly wondered 'if too much were not being expected of that young man'. There were also those people who considered that life in a wheelchair was simply not worth living at all. Many were consumed with aching pity for 'the girl whose life had been ruined'. All wholeheartedly admired the courage of the young couple, but behind many suitably bright smiles there was grave doubt of the future.

Against this image, invisible yet palpable, John made his polite speech of thanks to his new in-laws, to his own parents, to friends and acquaintances. He paused, and there was a short silence. He looked around the hall and leaned slightly forward, palms on the table.

'I know what you are thinking,' he said quietly, and the silence suddenly became intense. 'You are wondering about the future, and what on earth life as a paraplegic must be like.

'Well, we've decided to let you into a few secrets.

'First of all, paraplegia doesn't mean that you sit at home twiddling your thumbs, waiting for something to happen. Not at all.

'Secondly, it doesn't mean you have a little servant bustling around to attend to your every requirement.

'There is no question of my being a nursemaid,' he said deliberately, and waited for the effect of his words to sink in.

'It is quite unnecessary, as Margaret is quite capable of undertaking all activities of daily living. No doubt you've already observed this.

'On the other hand, paraplegia does mean that we plan ahead as much as possible—but we are of course still able to enjoy the unexpected. You see, planning can be quite good fun. We know that our plan *has* to work, and better still, that we are going to execute it. We feel that planning will be a most invigorating pastime in our life together.

'In addition, we still believe that there is no such word as "can't"; everything we might wish to do merely needs to be approached with true thinking to determine ways and means of achievement. We're quite prepared to admit that there are some things we won't be able to do in the usual conventional way— well, we'll simply do them in some other way. Take for example, swimming, which I suppose we can say is the art of self-propulsion in water, and usually done with arms and legs. But—it can be readily undertaken by the use of arms only. But that is only one small example. I can assure you that we intend to plan and meet *all* circumstances; we are going to take full part in life's activities —*and we fully expect to enjoy it!*

'In concluding these remarks I suppose our overriding thought is how much we appreciate your sincere good wishes for our future happiness—I know it has given us a great start together. And I know you'll agree with me when I say that I've been fortunate in finding such a wonderful person as—my wife—'

At the two magic words the tension dissolved in a storm of applause and laughter.

John was completely unaware of what he had just achieved in the field of public relations—on the subject of rehabilitation of the disabled into the community. For, during his speech, the sombre grey image on the invisible screen had wavered, dissolved, and finally vanished, to be replaced by the warm, glowing colours of joyous faith.

Gerta's sister Margaret was married to Tom Jensen, a mining

110

engineer, whose work over the years had necessitated moving the family many times from State to State. At present he was employed at Yallourn, a famous town in the fertile Latrobe Valley district, built by the State electricity commission for the winning of brown coal and the production of power and briquettes. Margaret had stayed there many times, and as a student of architecture she was particularly interested in the well-designed public buildings and gardens. It was to Yallourn that she made her first overnight visit away from Melbourne since leaving hospital. The Jensens had never had a home of their own in over twenty years of marriage. Tired of the constant adapting to rented places, they had at last built a beautiful house at Merricks, a quiet and lovely country district on a central ridge of hills in the Mornington Peninsula. Here they planned to retire some day. In the meantime it was used by the family during weekends and holidays. It was an ideal spot for two young people on their honeymoon.

Here Margaret and John discovered that the happiness of being together compensated a thousandfold for the inconveniences of paraplegia. A honeymoon was meant to be enjoyed; they revelled in every minute. They had private barbecues, picnics, and drives along the coast in the family car, which Gerta and John had lent them. When it rained they talked contentedly for hours, making endless plans for the future. They had little money, they had neither of them completed their university courses, they still lacked a suitable place to live—but they felt that as long as they were together nothing was too difficult to achieve.

It was during those long quiet talks that Margaret learnt to know and appreciate her young husband in a way that had not been possible during the busy days of their courtship at the University, or in the difficult months after the accident.

John had stayed for a time with the Watkins family after his discharge from hospital, while Margaret was still in the Spinal Centre. With the Lester family car all smashed, travelling to and from his own home in the outer suburb of Blackburn was too difficult. At Ryeburne Avenue he would often come in quietly after visiting Margaret, and go silently to the piano. There he would sit until late into the night playing Beethoven, Bach, or Schubert; what went on in his mind during those hours nobody knew. His musical talent was inherited from both parents. His father had eight brothers and sisters, every one of whom played a

111

musical instrument. Music was in his blood. He played both organ and piano, the latter with a gentle, sensitive touch that matched the general impression he gave of quietness and steadiness. His romance with Margaret was an attraction of opposites. She had been embarrassed on that first outing when the whole family had descended riotously on her escort; she did not then realize how fascinated he had been by the Watkins' ability to create excitement and the happy sense of adventure. It was precisely these characteristics that he loved in Margaret. About her physical disabilities he was as realistic as she was—both of them considered that other things were more important. Neither wanted to lead a shallow, empty life; they were interested in the world around them, they wanted to make their own positive contribution, and they intended to enjoy every minute.

'Why not?' he had snapped tersely when someone asked if he were still going to marry Margaret now that she was in a wheelchair. 'She's the same person, isn't she, except that she can't use her legs?'

As for Margaret, without John, what would have been the point of striving to rehabilitate herself? How would she fare without his help and encouragement? She knew too many paraplegics who, courted before disaster overtook them, were deserted afterwards.

'The desertion was ten times worse than the paraplegia,' one had told her.

Margaret was perfectly well aware of her good fortune in having John Lester for her husband.

Everyone knows that honeymoons have to come to an end. All too soon the Lesters had to return to Melbourne. John went off to earn the daily bread, and Margaret, like many other brides, found to her surprise and dismay that marriage involved spending a large part of every day on her own, but without the delights of managing a fascinating new home. Indeed, they had been lucky to find anywhere at all to live that was within their means. At one stage, just before the wedding, when it looked as if they were going to be homeless, John had said philosophically, 'Well I guess that when we come back from Merricks I'd better go home to my parents and you to yours, until we do find a suitable place.'

'What a darned silly idea!' exploded Margaret. 'What's the use of getting married and then getting separated again? Wherever we go it's got to be together.'

'All right, don't get into a twit. I was just trying to be helpful.'

In the end they answered an advertisement and found a tiny room in Tooronga Road, Malvern, in a house owned by a kindly Salvation Army woman. Thankful to have a roof over their heads, they locked up the borrowed house at Merricks, regretfully returned the car, and settled into their first home.

Its furniture consisted mainly of an enormous old-fashioned iron double bedstead, complete with brass bars, curlicues and jangling springs. It was so high that Margaret had to use almost super-human strength to transfer to it from her wheelchair—with a little imagination, its response could have been scored for symphony orchestra. The other essential item was a commode chair which Margaret loathed but was forced to use because it was quite impossible to get her wheelchair into the toilet, owing to the plan of the house; she could only use the latter if John were at home to assist her. For the same reason she could only bath at night when he was there to help. With bed and commode chair dominating the room, there was scarcely room for anything else. As it was, she could barely manoeuvre her wheelchair in the space that remained.

Shopping made a diversion; she enjoyed bowling along in her wheelchair and carrying the things home in her lap. Sometimes, if she needed to buy more extensively, she would order a taxi to the shopping centre at Camberwell Junction, getting the driver to put the wheelchair in the boot. These were grand occasions— even the time when she dropped a large bottle of cider and it smashed at the taximan's feet—but they had to be kept to a minimum. Money was tight. Margaret was no spendthrift. She hoarded every penny she could.

But in spite of shopping and housekeeping the days often seemed very long. She was able to get into her landlady's kitchen, which she was sharing; it meant she could prepare their meals. To fill in more time she began to spend hours baking cakes. Her landlady's dear old father sometimes wandered in, attracted by the delicious smells.

Best of all were the days when Gerta bustled in, arms full of surprises, from dress patterns to bags of fruit, with all the latest news of family and friends. None of the brothers and sisters were

113

free to visit in the daytime. Natalie was teaching; the others were at school. Gerta was full of plans for the Watkins' latest scheme, to move house once more. They had transferred to Hawthorn when the family had threatened to burst the walls of their former house. Now that their numbers were shrinking again, Gerta was finding it too much for her strength. The doctor had ordered her to curtail her activities; she and John were looking for a smaller place, easier to run, and farther away from the city. Somewhere near trees and hills. She did not tell Margaret another reason; the Hawthorn house would forever be associated with the pain and grief of those early terrible months after the accident. She wanted to put it all behind her.

'I only hope someone will buy it before we go to the beach at Christmas; if they don't, someone may have to stay behind. What are you and John doing? Would you like to live at Ryeburne Avenue while we're at Lorne?'

'That would be fabulous! It's nice here but it does get a wee bit cramped,' confessed Margaret.

'Why don't you let it go, darling? Ryeburne Avenue will give you a breather to look for somewhere else.'

It was wonderful to be in familiar, comfortable surroundings again, with only John for company. Margaret sighed with relief as she was able to resume her cherished independence in toilet routines. She could also wheel herself easily along the big ramp whenever she needed to leave the house.

'This is terrific!' she told John as she served his meal in Gerta's roomy kitchen. 'The only snag is that the agent keeps bringing people to inspect the house, so I have to keep every corner of it tidy! They always seem to ring the doorbell when I'm not dressed. I have to tear around and grab a dressing-gown, or else make them wait while I put on my clothes.'

She put a plate of hot food in front of John, and began to pour coffee as the phone rang. He lifted the receiver.

'What is it?' she asked quickly, as she saw the expression on his face. 'Is anything the matter?'

'Not really,' he murmured. He said a few polite words to his caller, and replaced the receiver. He sat and looked at her intently without saying a word.

'Well, what is it? Who was it?'

'It was Dr Cheshire.'

Margaret nearly dropped the coffee pot.

'What did he say? Was it about those tests he asked for?'

'He said, quote, I want to congratulate you, John. You are going to be a father. End of quote. Don't look so stunned; we'd always planned to have a large family, hadn't we? Got to make a start some time.'

'But I *am* stunned.'

'Don't act like a girl in a book. You suspected it, didn't you?'

'Well—I knew it was possible. But it just seems so fantastic. Do you think everything will be all right?'

'Don't be a drip. Of course it will. Stop pouring the coffee all over the table and eat up your dinner. Remember we've got to take care of you now.'

Gerta had suggested that Margaret and John join the family for a beach holiday at Lorne, during John's brief summer vacation. As carefully as they planned every excursion nowadays, they arranged the itinerary. Margaret would do the packing, get herself, baggage and wheelchair into a taxi, meet John at Spencer Street Station in the city after his work, and ride in the guard's van the fifty miles to the railroad junction of Geelong, Victoria's second port, which is on Corio Bay. There they would transfer to John Watkins' big car and be driven the forty-odd miles around the coast to Lorne. All would have gone according to schedule had they not been given the wrong train information over the telephone. When Margaret arrived at the station, John Lester was frantically pacing up and down at the taxi rank. He seized the chair and the minute she had slid into it he began to load her with bundles.

'We've got to run like mad,' he informed her, grabbing the suitcases. 'Here—' He shoved an enormous beach hat on to her lap. 'Get cracking.' With John haring ahead to clear the way they tore along through the crowds. Margaret's hands pumped away at the wheels like pistons, the beach hat flapping and catching as she went.

'All aboard!' the guard was shouting as they shot through the barrier. He put the whistle to his mouth.

'Hey—wait for us!' shouted John.

They got themselves, wheelchair, bag and baggage into the guard's van just before the train pulled out.

'Heavens! My brakes!' exclaimed Margaret as the chair slid straight into a wooden packing-case. She secured it carefully. They relaxed, panting, while ships, bridges and smoking factories slid past, giving way to the backyards of suburban houses.

An hour or so later they spied John Watkins' tall figure and welcoming face among the crowd as the train pulled into Geelong station. Soon they were in his car, catching tantalizing glimpses of the bay as they passed through the city, which was lively with summer visitors. Leaving the town behind they drove along the pleasant country road between grey-green gum-trees. Then, coming into the little township of Anglesea from the top of a hill they suddenly saw river and bushland stretching away towards misty hills. Below them lay the ocean, and a sweep of golden sand dotted with colourful beach umbrellas and hundreds of people in gay swimsuits. Although it was early evening, it was still broad daylight and very hot.

'Look at that surf!' exclaimed Margaret. 'Wouldn't I like to be in it! Maybe if I put on my swimsuit you could push me into the water in my wheelchair and let the waves break over me. What do you think, John? I'll bet it would do me good.'

'The question is whether it would do the wheelchair good— but we'll have a shot at it anyway,' promised her husband.

The car had slowed down to pass through the swarms of people walking along the roadside, or crossing to and from the paths to the beach. It gathered speed a little as they swept up the hill and entered the Great Ocean Road. John Watkins drove as skilfully as he did nearly everything he undertook; here this was a necessity, for the road, comparatively narrow, and used by hundreds of cars, was not an easy one. Curving constantly, it snaked its way around the edge of tall cliffs, while on the left there was a sheer drop to the jagged black rocks edging the sea. Since in Australia the driver sits on the right-hand side of the car and all traffic keeps to the left, nervous passengers on this road were often seen to have their eyes tightly shut. Margaret's were not: she was too absorbed in the breathless panorama of ocean and sky, one of the most magnificent seascapes in the Southern Hemisphere.

At last they reached their destination. Lying between hills and ocean, every landmark familiar in the evening sunshine, Lorne was, if anything, even more crowded than Anglesea had been. Luckily the Watkins had a rented cottage where they could do as they pleased. The family was waiting, and the Lesters were given a rapturous welcome.

'We nearly missed the train. I'm still in a tizzy!' said Margaret, when the kisses and hugs were over.

'That's because of your interesting condition,' teased Natalie.

'Let's go to the Arab for a meal, and get Ian and Phillip to wait on us,' suggested Gerta.

They all surged into Lorne's favourite eating-place, where the young Watkinses had taken holiday jobs waiting on customers and helping in the kitchen. Margaret had worked there herself the year before. It was an ideal place for young romantics, dimly lit, with interesting stonework and striped awnings. At the back of the restaurant those who wished could sit on the floor on cushions and eat at low tables. The place was always packed with young people in gay beach clothes. It was Margaret's first visit since her accident, and it was quite a triumphant procession, with everyone calling greetings and cheerfully moving aside to let the wheelchair through.

'What are you people going to have?' asked Ian with a grin, flourishing the menu. He was looking remarkably handsome in his T-shirt and okanuis. Several female customers were eyeing him appreciatively.

A handsome, barefooted Italian bustled out of the kitchen, a teatowel knotted round his waist. He was Reno, the chef. 'Margaret! Welcome back! It is wonderful to see you. What are you going to have? Ravioli? Spaghetti? Capuccino? And a Harem Girl for dessert?'

Margaret privately shuddered at the thought of eating rich food. She chose the plainest item on the menu and sat back contentedly. 'Isn't this heavenly?' she beamed. Life seemed completely perfect to her at that moment, surrounded by the family she loved, John at her side, the knowledge of her coming baby glowing within her. She felt she would never desire another thing in her whole life.

Gerta was unusually quiet. So often she felt wretchedly unwell these days. Packing and transporting the family had been exhausting. Once she would have taken it in her stride.

'We nearly didn't get here at all,' commented John Watkins. 'I had to work late every night—thanks to the Electras.'

'What's going to happen?' asked John Lester. 'Or is it top secret? They found some structural defects in the machines, didn't they?'

'Yes. It's no secret. Lockheed's have decided to make some modifications to the planes, so all our Electras, and Ansett's too, will be going over to Los Angeles to be altered. It will take about four weeks for each one in turn.'

'Are they taking passengers?'

'Not in the ordinary sense, but we'll carry a few TAA staff on leave; they'll just pay out-of-pocket expenses. No TAA wives, though, much to Mum's sorrow.'

Margaret's eyes were sparkling. 'Dad, I've never been to America! Do you think I could go?'

'Well, that's certainly an idea, isn't it?' answered her father. 'I guess we could make an exception to the staff rule in your case. But I'm not too sure if the facilities would suit a paraplegic, under the circumstances. It's worth looking into.'

'What would we use for money?' grinned John Lester.

'You couldn't go unless you were sure of staying in some place that would accommodate a wheelchair,' commented Natalie.

'Darling, you've got to take care of that baby,' said Gerta gently.

'Don't be disappointed,' John Lester said. 'Wait till I can take you myself.'

They all regarded her sympathetically.

'I can just see it all,' she exclaimed. 'It's going to be absolutely fabulous. Mum, I'll be able to buy Junior's first clothes in America!'

The Director of the Spinal Injuries Centre looked at one of Melbourne's leading obstetricians, and they nodded to each other.

'One of my patients went all round the world when she was pregnant,' said Professor Townsend, 'and she and the child are simply fine. If she can do it, so can Margaret.'

'Come to us for your injections,' invited Dr Cheshire. 'We'll look after you. Anything else we can do?'

'Could you give me a certificate or something to say I'm house-trained?'

'If you put it that way—yes, I can. Is this a prerequisite for entering the States?'

'Well, no, but it is for going on the plane. They won't take me if they think I'm not fit to look after myself.'

'No fear of that! Where are you going to stay?'

'I don't know yet. Dad's writing to someone he knows in Los Angeles, to see what they can suggest. The trouble is, we haven't got any money.'

Dr Cheshire smiled. 'I doubt if a little thing like that will stop you,' was his comment.

When any of the Watkins family undertook a project that most other people would have rejected as being impossible, difficulties had a habit of melting like butter on a hot scone. People were constantly being surprised at the family's undertakings; the more so because they were usually successful. If, as occasionally happened, a plan misfired, at least the Watkins had a great deal of fun out of it, for their usual reaction in such a case was laughter. Perhaps the secret of their successful living was whole-heartedness —what Charles Morgan termed the 'flashing stream': single-mindedness, to which was added enthusiasm. Gerta had once set off to join her husband overseas at a week's notice, having in the meantime let the house, arranged for the care of four children and a dog in several different places, and organized finance, taxation clearance, passage by sea, and her own travelling requirements. Once the family had endorsed Margaret's determination to go to America, pregnant, paraplegic and impecunious, it was merely a matter of arranging the details and, as usual, paths began to open before them.

John Watkins had written to Tom Bergmann, a friend in the Lockheed Company in California, to ask if he could suggest some organization or hostel which could provide suitable accommodation for a paraplegic. To his astonishment he received a letter back saying that Tom Bergmann's company had just arranged to make his services available for a time to Community Chest. John was well acquainted with this nation-wide organization, which includes paraplegics among the thousands of people it helps; his friend would be in daily contact with just the people who knew precisely the sort of place Margaret would need. Tom's letter was in due course followed by one from Rosemary Kolde, the Director of

119

Professional Services at Casa Colina, a rehabilitation centre for the physically handicapped situated about twenty-nine miles from Los Angeles.

'We would be very happy to have your daughter stay at our new Centre,' wrote Mrs Kolde. 'We feel her stay here would be mutually beneficial, since we would like to know more about the rehabilitation of paraplegics in your country. We have a complete new centre in Pomona, and we are anxious to make it the most modern and best of its kind. Your daughter could aid us in this by telling of her experience in rehabilitation in Australia.'

This exciting letter put the whole American adventure into a different perspective, not only because it would solve the financial problem, but because it would fulfil a serious purpose. Margaret Lester would now go as an ambassador for Australia, and for the rehabilitation methods which Dr Cheshire was carrying out so successfully at the Austin's Spinal Injuries Centre. Simply by being the person she was, she would encourage disabled people in another country.

Clutching in her hot hand this proof that she would be neither homeless nor destitute during her visit, Margaret was able to obtain Uncle Sam's Melbourne signature to all the necessary documents.

Thence all was easy. Expenses for the trip were somehow scraped together. Natalie industriously stitched an attractive muu-muu. Armed with knitting wool for several baby-jackets, and a well-stocked writing case, Margaret set off alone for the United States.

ten | VISIT TO AMERICA

Dear Mum, Dad, Nat, Ian, Phil and Jo,*
Thank you one and all for *all* the things you did to help me on
my way. It's a truly wonderful trip, something I shall never forget.
We're due in at Burbank in four hours' time. I'm very excited.
The whole trip was very smooth, hardly a bump. Nat, your muu-
muu was just the thing for Hawaii. Every woman wears one in
Honolulu. There are many in the shops, but all too expensive.
I'll do my best to buy some material in the downtown area on
the way home. The styles I like best have puffed sleeves or are
sleeveless with a V neck in a contrasting colour. Many are worn
full length.

Mum, the baby wool is very handy. I've started the second front
of a cardigan and plan to knit a jumper and pixie hood as well.
The sticky heat and rich green undergrowth struck me at Fiji,
also the number of Indians. Apparently they go to Fiji on some
land settlement scheme. Hordes of children gathered round the
chair whilst we tootled around Nandi village. I love the fuzzy-

---

* These extracts are quoted from the original letters.

121

haired Fijian women with flowers in their hair and colourful frocks. All the people seemed to pad around in bare feet, and smiled continuously, especially when they saw the chair. We stayed at the Mocambo Hotel.

The Reef, at Honolulu, is a wonderful hotel. I really enjoyed my swim in the pool and the drive around town. The others from the plane had all vanished so I asked a nice Canadian to lift me into the water and out again. Some of us hired a car and drove around town. Found the houses interesting. Noted the Japanese influence, and stained timber. Loved wandering around the International market at night, with the spotlighted palms, flares for lights, and bamboo sidewalk shops. American choc ice-cream is super. Sat down at tables there to drink in the atmosphere. Big, flashy cars seemed to be everywhere. I think they are too big. The taxi driver told me they are starting to have parking space problems, no wonder. Don't they glide along! Only spent $4.50 in Honolulu. How's that for economy? This included taxi, stamps, letter forms (18 of them), ice-cream.

Mr M. has given me his card. He will contact me towards the end of the week about coming to their home. He has done most of the lifting into the toilet etc. . . .

Guess what—Dr O'Donnell arranged for leis at the airport. I had three. Two of mauve orchids and one of a pink and white lily with a spicy perfume. I hope my pictures came out. So far have only taken three, one at Fiji and two of the party with their leis. (One with me in it.)

Good luck with your rowing, boys. Do let me know how it's going. . . .

24/3/61

Hello from Casa Colina, Pomona, California! Yes, I am actually here! The Administrator sent one of the executive officers to meet me in a car driven by their chauffeur. The officer is a gorgeous young lass called Mary Lou Ginther with a terrific American accent. I laughed at hers and she laughed at mine. We drove along the freeway to Casa Colina, about thirty miles, I would think. The freeway is very exciting at night. The lights are fantastic. They gave me a two-bed ward to myself. It's very comfortable except that I'm not used to the sealed windows and full air-conditioning. It feels stuffy at night when you're used to fresh air.

Next day the Administrator took me into his office, explained everything and got someone to take me on a conducted tour of the place. He's called the Administrator—he isn't the doctor-in-charge. They don't seem to have an overriding Medical Superintendent as we do. This is a truly magnificent building. It's a fabulous place altogether, newly built, and it isn't quite full yet. They have everything you can imagine for rehabilitating purposes —gymnasium, swimming pool, occupational therapy department, classroom, library. The swimming pool has a fabulous hydraulic hoist so that paraplegics can get in and out of the water without being lifted. Everything is most beautifully finished. Most of the patients seem to be children. All kinds of disabilities. I've spoken to two paraplegics and one quad so far. There's a little negro paraplegic about eleven years old. The quad is very depressed, he has children to support and doesn't know how he'll manage. I tried to cheer him up.

Everyone here is expected to try and walk. They think it's very important but I don't agree with that.

I just can't believe how well things are working out. It's hard to know where to begin telling you my impressions and outings. At the moment I'm dressed in your muu-muu, Nat, waiting to be picked up by Mrs Opie, a nurse here. She is taking me to a Hawaiian party. She spent most of today driving me around Claremont and Chino. Saw many orange groves, ranches, colleges, visited a drug store and supermarket. It was a cool foggy day with some light rain. It's wonderful having the Viyella coat and maternity suit, Mum. The country here is surrounded by mountains. So 'pretty', a word used by Americans for all attractive things. Many people laugh and get quite a kick out of my Australian expressions. I have questions such as, 'Do you all speak English?' 'Have you met so and so, a friend of mine in Sydney?'!

On Thursday Marion Terry called. We visited the City of Diamond Bar Housing Estate (near Pomona) of new homes priced from $30,000 to $33,000, quite luxurious, beautifully carpeted and so well-fitted, with full air-conditioning and even fold-down scales in the bathroom. Personally I didn't like the furniture. It lacks simplicity. We then called for her friend Millie and went for a drive to Descanso Gardens in La Canada. They have thousands of camellia trees and hundreds of rose bushes, some of which even date back to the 1500s. On the way we gorged on Burger de Luxe at a Drive In Restaurant. Millie had a cute little plastic seat for carrying her baby in the car and feeding him on a table. It may be useful for me. Cost about $6.50.

The Occupational Therapist here is lending me her muu-muu pattern. I hope to make one before returning home, to wear in Honolulu. Marion will take me shopping some time near the end of my stay. I can't wait. Mum, where is the best place to see Hawaiian dancing in Honolulu?

28/3/61

It certainly is exciting seeing new places, people and things. The weather is still just like Melbourne. Grey sky, intermittent rain, and I can see snow on the mountains behind Pomona. The first Californian sun for me shone at Torrance last Saturday. Evan Terry collected me in his little sports car. We hared along the freeway. This freeway travelling is so very amazing, cars, cars everywhere, and such speed. Marion took me to the local Masonic Hall where a luncheon and fashion parade was held. The girls' Youth Club, Job's Daughters, ran the show. That afternoon I went to the local supermarket to help Marion shop for food. Nat, I bought you some undies—luckily they had a table of specials, total cost about $3.50.

Yesterday we went to Exposition Park, had a brief look at the Museum, an old place rather like Melbourne's Museum. Also a fabulous new regional library at Arcadia, a superb new building, not yet officially opened. An assistant librarian gave us a conducted tour.

I showed Dad's colour slides to the hospital kids through the viewer. We are planning a proper screening so that most of the patients can look at them.

Stayed the night at Terrys', and today we go to Marineland and shopping. I adore the ice-cream, 31 different kinds. Had Rocky Road yesterday, chocolate with marshmallow and nuts.

Last Sunday Mrs Grady took me to her home in San Marino for lunch and tea. Such a pretty district. Her four kids and their extra friends produced a mad raucous household similar to ours at Ryeburne Avenue. She apologized, but I said, 'It's just like home.' Most enjoyable.

We drove through downtown Los Angeles to Beverly Hills, Pacific Ocean, University of Los Angeles and pretty canyon residential areas nearby.

Jo, Kathie Terry has some unusual jacks. I plan to get some for you.

4/4/61

Heartiest congratulations, Ian and Phil on your respective victories in the Scotch Mercantile Regatta. You must be on top of the world! You've no idea how disappointed I am not being able to see you in the rowing races. All the best for Head of the River and for your training. The eldest girls here thought you looked terrific in Dad's colour slides. They said, 'Send your brothers to Los Angeles next time!' I plan to buy the different varieties of gum for you boys, also some records.

I went to the Bucks for Easter. Mr Buck used to be in the meat industry. His firm imported Australian beef for hamburger meat here in America! They live in a super upstairs apartment in South Pasadena with lovely gardens and tree-lined streets. They had a traditional Easter lunch. Their three-year-old twin grandchildren had an Easter-egg hunt in the garden. . . . I picked up some interesting food tips. Ham served with banana sauce (yummy) (vitamized banana, lemon juice, touch of horse-radish and cream). Sweet potatoes with cinnamon, eggs poached in butter and sour cream on a layer of cheese. Barbecued steak marinaded in soya sauce and other spices. . . . Here at Casa Colina the children all had new clothes and eggs and Easter bunnies. I will buy my white Easter bonnet tomorrow.

Yesterday Mr May collected me. We met an architect, Mr Russell, at his office. Later I lunched at Burbank then went to the Mays' home for dinner. It was 110° in the Burbank area, and today it's 90°. The worst part of driving in heat is the smog, it makes your eyes feel so gratey. Will go to San Diego for a few days next week. Marion Terry will take me there.

9/4/61

. . . On Friday morning I set off with Mr Cunnison, Administrator for Casa Colina, to Pomona Bus Terminal. Greyhounds refused to issue me a ticket as I would have to change buses at Los Angeles for San Diego. Drivers may injure backs assisting handicapped people!! A real blow to my independence. Felt a bit diffident about asking for assistance with bus at San Diego Zoo. However, the driver gave a broad smile, lifted me into seat, 'at your service, ma'am.' My faith in Americans is restored. Eventually caught Santa Fe train at Fullerton, disembarked at Del Mar. Mr Cunnison arranged for Bill, the Casa Colina driver, to help me on to train. The Walcotts met me. Isn't their home a dream? La Jolla is a beautiful district. In fact San Diego appeals to me far more than Los Angeles. Love the views from Point Loma. Dined at a superb Chinese restaurant, then yesterday lunched at the Chuck Waggon, smorgasbord style. Today we visited the Zoo and Balboa Park. Lunched at the restaurant. A fabulous Zoo, isn't it? Saw some beautiful orchids and Easter lilies in the greenhouse. Still find it staggering to see so many gum-trees.

Lisa Walcott (4½) is cute. She follows me everywhere asking questions about junior and about wheelchair. . . .

Bought some terrific bargains. . . .

Los Angeles

. . . A friend . . . and her architect husband will drive me to Sherman Oaks for a luncheon party. . . . Thursday Marion will collect me for a trip to Disneyland, mustn't miss that.

As far as I know the plane will leave 7 a.m. Saturday morning . . . thanks for tip about Hawaiian dancing. I will certainly go there for dinner. . . .

My love to everyone,

Margaret.

She was on her way home again after a dream holiday. She leaned back in the comfortable plane seat—one of the few chairs that were suitable for her because of the armrests—and gazed out of the window at the ocean many miles below. It had all been such fun. She had done everything she had set out to do and really it had been easy, thanks to so many good friends. She had even managed, on the way home, to bathe in the breakers at famous Waikiki beach. Paraplegia needn't stop anyone from doing *anything* if they really wanted to do it badly enough. People spent so much time worrying about things that didn't matter.

126

As she dreamed she felt a faint stirring within her, the delicate, yet unmistakable movement of her child. Suddenly a wave of panic swept over her. Supposing something happened. Supposing the plane crashed, or she developed a 'skin-off', or one of those swift, terrible infections to which every paraplegic is prone. Supposing she couldn't get back to John ever! For the rest of the journey she was in a fever of impatience. The weeks behind dissolved into the nebulous past. Nothing mattered, nothing was real, nothing was stable until the plane touched down in Melbourne. They carried her down and put her into her wheel-chair. Hands going like pistons, she sped across the tarmac to a wildly excited Watkins family—and John Lester.

eleven || MOTHERHOOD

Margaret and John had managed to rent a small house, one of a terrace in Newry Street, Carlton. The front door, only a few feet from the footpath, opened on to a narrow passage with rooms on the left. The passage led to a small kitchen on the same level, but there was a steep step down to the tiny bathroom. The men of the family constructed a ramp to go over this, and a wooden frame to raise the level of the toilet seat., There was a shower over the bath. John nailed two pieces of wood across the front and back legs of an ordinary wooden kitchen chair to make a shower seat that would fit inside the bath without slipping. It was not an entirely satisfactory arrangement, but it worked. The house was ready for a paraplegic. True, Margaret could only use the bathroom by wheeling in frontways and reversing back up the ramp, no other movement being possible; the laundry was inaccessible; and she could only glimpse the miniature back garden from inside the house, since there was no ramp. But she was independent. Moreover, the house was within wheeling distance of Melbourne University, where she had undertaken to tutor in Building Construction—and the young Lesters had no car. Margaret

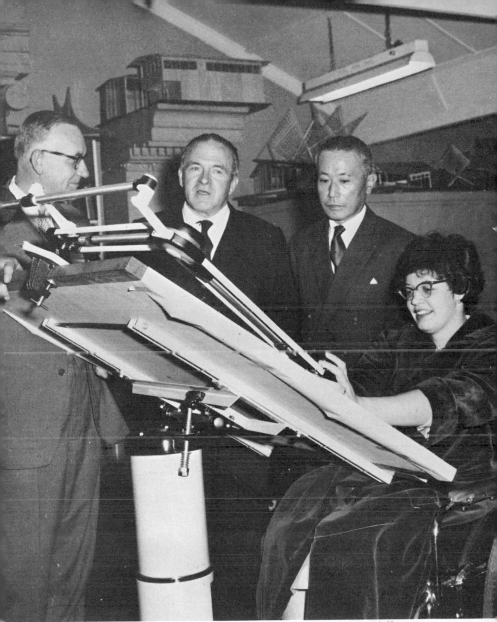

Age, Melbourne

Trying out the mechanical drawing-table and drawing-machine designed for disabled people and presented to the University of Melbourne by Mutoh Drafter Industries Ltd, Tokyo. *Left to right*: Mr J. A. Zwarteveen, Company Agent, Professor Brian Lewis, Mr Katashi Suga, Japanese Consul-General, and Margaret

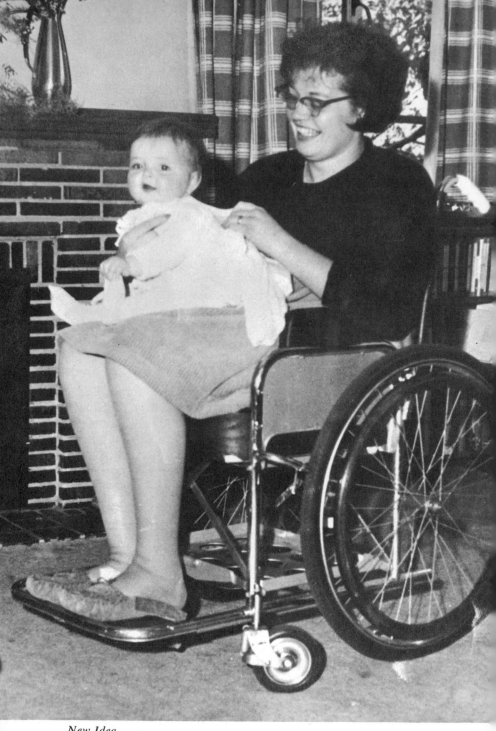

New Idea

Dressing Cindy

enjoyed the tutoring. The students worked individually at drawing boards; it was easy to wheel among them to inspect and advise.

Still glowing from her American adventure, she enthusiastically took up the routine of housekeeping, university work and preparations for the baby. Before long, however, she had a setback, one of the ever-present threats to the paraplegic: accidental abrasion or excessive pressure on the skin of hips or seat, producing the dreaded 'skin-off'. She was ordered into hospital until it was healed.

It was Ward Eighteen again, only this time she was in a six-bed room. Three of the patients were usually up and working in the Occupational Therapy Department. The remaining three, including Margaret, were in bed.

She lay impatiently staring at the empty bed opposite. There was a small plastic fan on the floor beside it, which she fancied she had seen twirling around. Now it did not appear to be moving. She watched it idly. Gerta's friendly voice came from the other end of the ward where she was talking to another patient.

Suddenly there was a puff like a cracker from the overheated fan, followed by a series of loud popping noises and a strong smell of burning. Smoke began to eddy through the room. It was a situation that Margaret had sometimes visualized during her time in the Acute Ward. Now it was actually happening, and for the first time in her life she experienced real panic. There was not a wheelchair in sight. She knew that she and the other two bed patients were helpless without them.

'Bring me my chair!' she called loudly.

By now the others were calling out too, completely terrified.

The smell of burning increased as the bedcover caught fire. She heard Gerta running out of the ward for help. Within seconds a nurse was there, smothering the burning fan and bedcover with a blanket, and almost immediately the ward was full of people.

The whole episode was over in a matter of minutes and the only one who was any the worse was the nurse, who had burnt her hand. But Margaret continued to tremble. Most times she faced life with cheerful confidence, paraplegia or no paraplegia. Once, when she had fallen out of her wheelchair, she had simply lain quietly on the floor, knowing that in a few hours John would be home. She could not get herself from floor level into the wheelchair; in any case she would have hesitated to try the experiment lest she should fall and injure her unborn baby. Another time when she had fallen in the front hall she had waited to ask the postman for help. In the Carlton house the letters were poked under the front door—she only hoped that there would be some mail for the Lesters that day; and fortunately there was. But just occasionally, as now, she was rudely jerked into realizing that in certain situations she would be helpless indeed. It always worried her in public auditoriums, where, once she had transferred to a seat, her wheelchair was usually whisked away to leave the aisle free. What would she do if a fire broke out there? She found that many other paraplegics shared the same private fears.

Discharged again from hospital, Margaret determined that at least no neglect of hers should be responsible for the next inevitable skin-break. With fanatical vigilance she carried out the daily inspection of her body with a long-handled mirror, trying to spot the warning signs of red patches before they could develop any further. It was infuriating, therefore, when Professor Townsend, her obstetrician, ordered her back into hospital for other reasons.

'Is there something wrong with my baby?' she asked in alarm.

'I didn't say that at all. I would say that the baby is fine, as far as we can tell. But your blood pressure is not, and there are a couple of other little things. We can't afford to take any risks with a paraplegic patient, Margaret. You know that. Let's see, we plan to deliver the baby by caesarian section in exactly a month's time. The child needs every minute of that month. I think you should go straight to bed and stay there from now on. Can you admit her?' he asked Dr Cheshire.

'Of course. She can stay here right now and phone John to come in tonight and bring in anything she needs.'

'John's lecturing tonight,' protested Margaret. 'He never has a free evening. And anyway, we planned to go to Merricks this weekend. My auntie has a fabulous house down there. It's the one where we spent our honeymoon. It's so hard for John to get away. We've been planning this weekend for ages.'

'Well then,' said Professor Townsend, 'I'll let you have your Roman holiday, seeing it's already planned, but you must come straight back into hospital, right?'

'Right,' groaned Margaret, as the doctors nodded and walked away.

130

The weekend at Merricks successfully banished all gloomy thoughts. When it was over, however, and Margaret was installed once more in bed in the Spinal Centre, she felt she simply could not endure a month of inactivity and hospital routine. John's evenings were fully occupied with university lectures and army training. She had to wait several days before she could explode her indignation in his sympathetic ear. The patients had long since been settled down for the night when he eventually arrived, weary after a day's work, evening lectures, and a journey by public transport from Carlton to Heidelberg. He was no sooner at her bedside than one of the night staff appeared, scolded him for visiting so late, and told him he could not stay.

'Well then, I just won't be able to come and see you,' he said, 'because I'm working every night, and without a car I can't get here any earlier.'

He kissed her goodbye and set off philosophically enough on the tiring journey home. Margaret was furious.

'If John's not coming to visit me, then I *won't* stay,' she told herself. Reaching out for the book she had brought, she lay reading it the entire night. The Night Sister came in several times to offer a warm drink, but she refused, doggedly continuing to plough her way through Xavier Herbert's *Capricornia*.

In the morning Dr Cheshire appeared.

'Now, Margaret, what's all this about? You're supposed to be resting.'

'I can't rest if I don't know how John's getting on, and never see him. I ought to be at home.'

He thought for a moment. 'If you could find someone to keep an eye on you, and if you would promise faithfully to do exactly what you were told—'

'I would—if I could only go home.'

'You might try getting a council housekeeper. If you can tee something up by phone I'll let you go.'

He was hardly out of the ward before Margaret was in her wheelchair racing to the telephone. She already knew about the Home Help Scheme in which certain municipalities, subsidized by the Victorian Government, provided an emergency housekeeper where there was need. The fees charged to the householder were assessed according to his capacity to pay. Margaret thought she had a good chance of being considered for this service, and to

131

her great joy a council housekeeper was found. She was to come to the house until 2 p.m. every weekday.

Within hours Margaret was back in bed at Newry Street, her baby-sewing, knitting and writing materials at hand, telephone close by for organizing household needs and chatting to friends. In the tiny hall was one of her parents' silver-wedding presents, an electric food-warmer on wheels, which Gerta had lent her. As it had several compartments, a whole dinner could be prepared during the day and kept warm until it was time for the evening meal. Its correct name, John Watkins had insisted, was bain-marie, and he had looked it up in the dictionary to prove his point.

Margaret sighed with relief. Taking a writing pad from the bedside, she began to check once more the sizes and heights of her baby equipment. Everything had to be exactly right within inches when one was caring for a baby from a wheelchair.

'Look who's come to see you!' said Gerta, ushering in an eager three-year-old whose arms were clamped around a yellow baby-bath.

It was June's little boy Philip, usually known as little Phil, to distinguish him from others of the same name. He might have walked straight out of a Tyrolean landscape, with his velvet straps embroidered with edelweiss, his short black pants, long white socks, and green hat with a plume of feathers. It was his usual going-out costume, worn to please his Viennese-born father.

'This is the bath I had when I was a little boy,' he informed Margaret. 'You can have it for your baby. Where is your baby?'

'Thank you. Give me a kiss. The baby'll be coming soon.'

'Shall we wait for it?' He turned to his mother, who was standing in the doorway with a baby-basket under each arm. There was no space to put them down.

'Not today. Another day we'll come to see it.'

'What a beautiful hat!' said Gerta to the child.

'Would you like to see the feathers? Look, a green one, a yellow one, a red one and a purple one.' He spied the bain-marie in the narrow hallway. 'What's that?'

'That's for keeping Margaret and John's dinner hot.'

'How does it work?'

'I'll show you,' said Gerta. She smiled at him lovingly, holding

132

out her hand towards him. He put his own little hand into hers and they went off happily together.

For some reason the incident made a deep impression on his mother. Later she was to recall every detail.

June was one of Gerta's closest friends. A favourite music pupil of the aunt after whom Gerta was named, Gertrude Carey, she had always been accepted as a member of the family; sometimes Gerta absentmindedly introduced her as 'my sister'. All the family loved her, and had accepted her as a frequent member of their lively household from the time when the children were little. She joined in their activities, baby-sat at times, and shared her music with them. At Gerta's request she had amplified for the girls their mother's information about the birds and the bees, because, Gerta had said vaguely, 'you would naturally be able to explain about the diagrams and things'. How Gerta linked this subject with musicianship might not have been clear to some people, but she and June understood each other perfectly. No one but Gerta would have brought her, when she was playing at a concert, a fresh young cauliflower in the circlet of its own green leaves, because it looked so much prettier than a bunch of flowers; no one but June could have received it with such delight.

June's romance with Julius had developed to a large extent in the Dean Avenue house, to the enormous and round-eyed interest of the children. She had been married from their home, dressed as a bride by Gerta, with Natalie as bridesmaid, and Margaret decorously excited in a new blue dress and matching bobble-trimmed hat.

When little Phil arrived, after years which had brought tragedy to June and Julius, he was a special joy to them. He was one of those children who take such an immense delight in people, and life in general, that they make everyone else feel happy. To him it seemed a very good idea to lend one's outgrown things to a tiny new baby; it made a three-year-old feel really grown-up.

June took the two baskets over to the bed, where Margaret examined them at first critically, and then with approval.

'This light basket will be ideal for using in a car—which we hope to have when John's accident compensation money comes through. The heavier basket can sit on the little stand. That will make it just the right height. I like the bath—the curved edge

133

will make it much easier to grip. Goodness—everything's nearly ready. I can't believe it.'

The baby was to be born at the Jessie MacPherson Community Hospital in the city. Gerta was to take Margaret there the day before to settle in. It seemed strange to be going there instead of to the Austin. A thousand butterflies seemed to have settled inside Margaret; she began to count the hours instead of the days.

'My last night at home,' she told John with satisfaction, as the phone began to ring.

A moment later she replaced the receiver with exasperation. 'What do you know! Professor Townsend's got a special meeting or something, so I can't have the baby till a day later. Isn't that maddening!'

'Not to worry.'

'But I've told everyone to look in the paper the next day, and if they don't see a birth notice they'll think something's gone wrong.'

'It won't.'

'Are you going to pace the corridor while the baby is being born, like they always do in books?'

'Not me! I'm going off to work as usual and wait until they ring up with the glad news.'

'But you will come and see me in hospital the night before?'

'Of course, you silly crumb.'

When John arrived to see her after his day's work Margaret was upstairs in another ward. He had to wait until she was brought down on a trolley to her bed in the general ward on the floor below. He was furious to find that her wheelchair had been left upstairs, and went storming up to find it.

'Don't you ever let them do that again,' he said, pushing it up to her bedside. He knew how helpless she felt without it.

'Well, I won't be able to use it anyway,' she said ruefully. 'This bed's so high I haven't a hope of getting myself off it and I'm not going to keep asking people to help me.'

The Sister, who had overheard the conversation, paused to reassure her.

'Don't worry, Mrs Lester. There must be a lower bed tucked away somewhere. I'll see if I can find one by the time you are ready to get up. Just forget it for the moment.'

'Good luck for tomorrow,' said John as he kissed her goodbye. 'It'll all be over very quickly.'

'Dr Scrivenor—she's the anaesthetist—came in to see me. She says I don't really need an anaesthetic for the operation because I couldn't feel anything anyway, but they think it's better for me not to see what's going on, so they'll give me just a little.'

She was fully conscious next morning when they wheeled her out of the ward. If John did not see any point in prowling the corridors like the traditional expectant father, Gerta and John Watkins did. They hovered about waiting for her to appear, and waved vigorously as she was pushed into the operating theatre. It was an awe-inspiring place with its gleaming equipment and its medical team all gowned and masked.

Dr Scrivenor's eyes smiled at her reassuringly as she deftly slipped a needle into her wrist.

'We'll just put you to sleep for a while now.'

It seemed almost immediately that she heard the clatter of metal instruments being put into a sterilizer.

The anaesthetist was still smiling. 'You have a girl.'

'A girl,' Margaret echoed stupidly. 'Where am I?'

'Mr John Lester?' a voice was saying in the distance. 'Professor Townsend here. You have a fine girl. Congratulations!'

Full consciousness returned to Margaret. She had shed no tears over her broken spine or useless legs; now she wept as if she would never stop.

'For goodness' sake give me something to dry her eyes. Come on, Margaret—don't cry! The baby's beautiful, really she is.'

But Margaret was choking with sobs. All the frustrations, doubts, fears and joys of the past eighteen months seemed to be erupting together. She couldn't stop.

'I can't breathe!' she yelled frantically.

'Get her some nose drops, please, Sister.'

'Where's my baby? I want to see her,' hiccuped Margaret at last.

'You'll see her in a moment.'

Dr Kate Campbell had whisked the baby out of the room almost straight into Gerta and John Watkins.

'You wouldn't be Margaret Lester's mother! You have the most beautiful granddaughter. See, isn't she lovely? Look at her hair!'

'She's perfect!' breathed Gerta, feasting her eyes on the wide-eyed infant.

'She's the image of Margaret,' marvelled John Watkins.

They were reverently watching her being wheeled away when Gerta was seized and soundly kissed on both cheeks. It was Professor Townsend, still streaming with perspiration under his surgeon's cap.

'Margaret's going to be quite all right,' he said, wringing John Watkins' hand. 'I'm more than satisfied with the way things have gone. In fact there's no reason why she shouldn't have up to two more babies, if she wants them. She's a wonderful girl. Her attitude to the whole thing has been inspiring.'

Dr Cheshire joined them, beaming all over his face. 'You have a truly remarkable daughter. She's a real inspiration to my other patients at the Austin, especially over this business. It shows what an indomitable spirit can do.'

Margaret smiled faintly at them as she was wheeled out. Back in bed in the ward she drowsed happily. Whenever she opened her eyes she saw Gerta's smiling face, but she was too tired to speak. Gerta sat there quietly, but when John Lester came she slipped out of the ward so that the young parents could be alone when they were introduced to their new daughter.

It was 5th August 1961: just about a year and six months since Margaret had been admitted to the Spinal Injuries Centre following the accident.

A fortnight later the Jessie MacPherson Hospital was exchanged for the Queen Elizabeth Hospital for Mothers and Babies. Here, although somewhat distressed to find the toilets too narrow for her wheelchair, Margaret revelled in becoming acquainted with Lucinda Jane and learning how to care for her.

At last it was time to go home. A council housekeeper was engaged to help her from nine to two o'clock, for two weeks. Afternoons, and evenings when John was at lectures—which was very often—she would care for the baby alone.

'What'll I do if she howls? How will I know what's wrong? What if she gets a dirty nappy?' she thought nervously.

By squeezing most of the difficult tasks into the morning when the housekeeper was there, she managed somehow to cope with

136

the rest of the day. But when the fortnight came to an end and she found herself completely alone, it was a different story.

Her own personal toilet routines took endless time in the inconvenient house. Now she had also to cope with the demands of a hungry and incontinent little newcomer. She could get the wheelchair neither into the laundry to do the washing nor outside to hang it up. She had to manage with a hand basin, and leave everything for John to peg out when he came home. Sometimes he did not get in till late at night and forgot or was too tired. Sterilizing the bottles was a nightmare when one had to lean precariously from a wheelchair and manage heavy saucepans of boiling water on a stove which was exactly the wrong height. The ramp into the bathroom made it impossible to push the moses basket on its stand into a position where the baby could conveniently be cleaned up. Bathing Cindy became a main problem; Margaret couldn't balance well enough to lean over and fill the baby-bath from the bathroom taps. It had to be filled slowly and carefully at the cold tap in the kitchen, and the murderous hot water added to it from the kettle. Then she would carry it on her lap to the dining-room table, wheeling carefully so that it wouldn't slop over. Sometimes she almost panicked and longed for someone to take over, someone on two strong legs who could move about swiftly coping with everything so that she could just rest.

Gerta came often but was curiously reluctant to offer help. One day she brought a close friend, Freda Wrigley, to admire little Cindy. Margaret was exhausted and still behind with the household chores; John had gone off to work in yesterday's shirt because several times running they had forgotten about hanging out the washing. A pile of damp shirts had been waiting in the kitchen for several days.

'They'll all go mouldy,' she said anxiously. Money was still very tight—one didn't buy new shirts without a great deal of forethought.

'I'll hang them out,' said Freda at once, stubbing out her cigarette.

Gerta put a restraining hand on her arm. 'Don't waste time on shirts. You don't see Margaret very often these days.'

'It'll only take a minute!'

'No. Leave it—another few hours won't make much difference.'

Freda caught a look from Gerta and subsided.

On the way home she took her friend to task. 'Why wouldn't you let me help Margaret? It wouldn't have taken a minute. She's got enough to do.'

'She's got to work it out herself. She and John,' said Gerta composedly. 'I know you think I'm hard, but I've seen too many people who spend their lives depending on everyone else because they aren't physically strong. Or think they aren't. Margaret's life is difficult. But if once she gets into the habit of leaning on everyone around her, she's finished.'

'But I don't think Margaret would ever do that!' expostulated Freda. 'She's too independent by nature. And that's the way she's been brought up, too. I can't see that a little bit of help at a time like this would do any harm.'

'Yes it could. A lot of harm. Don't you see—they've *got* to work out their own pattern of living. Let John find out that his shirts have gone mouldy. He'll soon remember to hang them out for her. She can't keep turning to me for everything; it wouldn't be right. Besides,' she added casually, 'I mightn't always be around.'

| twelve | WHEELCHAIR HOME |

Cindy was such an adorable baby, John such a delightful companion, that Margaret would not have changed places with anyone in the world. Only sometimes at night she was so exhausted that it took an almost superhuman effort to get her unco-operative body on to the bed for a short night's rest. It was another monster double bed, fully the size of the previous one. As usual it took up most of the space in the room, leaving the bare minimum for the wheelchair and the baby-basket on its stand. Everything had to be kept within reach of her bed or her wheelchair. At night she managed by putting an electric water-heater, bottles, and nappies on the chest of drawers next to her pillow. She could then attend to the baby without getting out of bed herself.

The small house was so cluttered with furniture and baby equipment that it took considerable skill to navigate her wheelchair between the various obstacles. As the baby increased in size, so did Margaret's difficulties and fatigue. She did not yet realize or acknowledge her limitations. The climax came one day when she had filled the baby-bath at the kitchen tap and carried it in her lap into the living room. As she tried to lift it up on to the table, somehow it slipped and landed noisily upside down on the carpet.

She sat, drenched to the skin with water she could not feel, looking at the havoc around her. How on earth was she going to clean it up from a wheelchair? The soaking wet carpet—not their own, for the house was let furnished—would take days to dry out, particularly in cold, damp weather. Cindy was crying loudly with fright. Margaret felt like crying too. A domestic mishap like this could be the last straw.

She gathered up the baby, and as usual the soft, adorable little bundle filled her with almost unbearable happiness. But Cindy wriggled and fought; she hated having her warm face pressed against her mother's wet clothes. Margaret laughed, but the angry little face sobered her. She took a deep breath.

'It's no use risking an accident by trying to cope with everything myself and getting too tired,' she thought. 'The baby is really all that matters. She must have my full attention. Then I'll do what housework I can, and what I can't manage will jolly well have to be left undone. Blow it!'

She sat thinking and planning. She really ought to have help, she now realized, to relieve her of the heavy chores, so that she could concentrate on Cindy. And sooner or later they must find a larger, more convenient house.

She talked it over with John. Finances would stretch to some occasional help for a few hours. Margaret thought she knew where she could get a young Italian girl to come in once a week to do the heavy washing in the old-fashioned copper, and clean the floors. With a napkin service for Cindy, Margaret could cope with everything else.

The new plan, once put into operation, worked admirably, and they began to enjoy life once more instead of always feeling desperately tired.

John's third-party insurance had enabled them to buy a car, and at weekends they were now able to get out of the little house and visit friends.

'If we could get the car fitted with hand controls I could drive it myself and not be dependent on you,' she said to John. 'The Red Cross gives lessons to disabled drivers.'

But there was such a long waiting list that Margaret decided to learn privately. She did not find it at all difficult. Within a few short weeks she had the enormous satisfaction of being able to drive herself and Cindy wherever she liked. One of her first visits was to East Doncaster. Gerta and John had found the exact place they wanted, a small modern house set in rolling green orchard country with a distant view of mountain ranges on the skyline, from Mount Macedon right round to the Dandenongs. They had named it, appropriately, 'Blue Sky'.

'It's wonderful to be mobile!' exclaimed Margaret as she delegated to Gerta the privilege of lifting Cindy out of the basket.

The problem of house space, however, was becoming daily more acute, and the young Lesters decided to move as soon as Margaret's insurance money came through. They had no other financial resources.

'If I received stacks of money we could build a perfect wheelchair house,' said Margaret hopefully. 'There are always these stories in the newspapers about people getting fabulous sums in compensation for accidents.'

There were to be no fabulous sums to compensate for Margaret's paraplegia, however. The comprehensive insurance policy held by John's father clearly stated that the company would accept responsibility (beyond the statutory third-party limit of £2000 which then applied) if the person driving the car were doing so with the permission of the owner. Most of the public, including the Lesters, thought this gave financial protection in case of damages legally assessed as the result of any accident. What they did not know was that this clause, sometimes called the 'honour' clause, was not strictly enforceable under British law, although refusal to act according to the printed terms of the policy was almost unheard of. In effect, if an insurance company chose not to pay beyond £2000 when the insured owner was not actually in the car at the time of an accident, there was no legal means of compelling them to do so. Even if an injured third party were severely disabled for life it made no difference. Margaret had elected to go to court before a jury, claiming damages against the driver on the grounds of his negligence; she believed she had an unanswerable case. However, the Lesters' insurance company, a reputable and famous Australian one, had a surprise in store for them. They let it be known that if the case did go to court, and a judgment were given in Margaret's favour for substantial damages against the driver, then they would cover his liability to the extent

141

only of £2000. This would leave Margaret virtually no hope of recovering the balance by civil action from the driver—a student without means of his own. She was strongly advised under the circumstances to settle out of court. The sum she received was probably not one-third of the amount the court would have awarded. It was, in fact, ludicrous compared with £43,400 ($86,800) awarded in the same year to a woman who had lost three fingers of her left hand and sustained facial injuries.

Nevertheless, Margaret and John were so overjoyed to have sufficient funds to put a deposit on a house, and a small sum in the bank for a rainy day, that they did not worry over-much. 'It's weird to think we had no hope in the world of having our own home for years, and now we have achieved it because of the accident,' was Margaret's wry comment.

Margaret's father, however, was so shocked at the discovery of this legal loophole that he wrote a vigorous letter of protest to the press. It aroused a great deal of comment. An editorial was written on the subject, questions were asked in Parliament. Whether or not Margaret's experience had an indirect bearing on the case will never be known, but the fact remains that a few years later in Victoria the statutory third-party limit of £2000 compensation was removed.

In December, with the insurance money safely in the bank, the young Lesters began an intensive house-hunt. It was a disappointing business. So many of the houses they might have afforded were quite impossible for a wheelchair. Steps and stairs abounded; windows were too high, giving a seated person the feeling of being imprisoned; doorways were too narrow. Five minutes, or sometimes a single glance, and Margaret would know that a place would not do.

Near Christmas with its rush of activities they were almost exhausted, and ready to postpone the search until after their holiday. They had planned a camping trip over the Christmas break to christen the new car, and Margaret was spending hours shopping, sorting, and packing in preparation. She had everything almost ready when one day John rang in great excitement.

'Look, I've found a house! How about coming and having a look at it?'

'*No*. I've had it. It'll be no good anyway.'

'Hey! Come and see before you pass judgment.'

'Oh, all right.' Margaret unwillingly stowed Cindy and herself into the car, and sped over to a side street in North Balwyn.

John was there already. He waited impatiently while she transferred herself into her wheelchair, plopped Cindy, like a round Christmas pudding, into her lap and fastened a pink ribbon around the back of the chair, herself and the baby. This was to prevent Cindy from toppling off Margaret's lap while her hands were busy propelling the wheelchair. John went ahead of her into the driveway of the house.

'Look at this!' he said.

She surveyed it critically. It was a typical solid, red-brick suburban home with a tiled roof. 'Not architecturally exciting,' she commented, 'but it has a pleasant, open atmosphere. Big casement windows—I could see out. The garden setting is pleasant —we'd have to turn those flower beds into grass, unless you wanted to do some gardening.'

She was teasing him, because she knew that gardening was not a favourite hobby of cither of them. Men paraplegics often enjoyed gardening, which they could manage well with long-handled tools and narrow garden beds, but she herself felt that a wheelchair housewife and mother had enough to do.

The interior of the house was unoriginal but pleasant, and there was a wonderful oil heater which would solve several problems: comfort in winter, warmth without difficult chores for a paraplegic, a means of drying babies' clothes in wet weather.

'The steps at the front and down to the back verandah are an awful nuisance. We'd have to make some alterations, but I think it might do. It might do very well!' she exclaimed with rising excitement. 'Let's ask Mum and Dad what they think.'

Gerta and John came and saw the house. The senior Lesters came and saw it. They all thought it might do very well indeed.

But the young couple were so used to counting their pennies that when it came to the point they couldn't bring themselves to buy the house. Instead, they went away on their camping holiday and tried to forget it. They were driving to Lorne, where they would stay with John and Gerta, then along the coast to Warrnambool and on to Mount Gambier, pitching a tent or staying at motels.

By the time they had reached Warrnambool the decision which they had scarcely discussed again had crystallized in both their

143

minds. In the motel bedroom John put through a trunk call to Melbourne, and made an offer for the house. And then they began to panic in case someone else had got in first.

'You wouldn't believe all that junk could come out of one small house,' marvelled John.

An army of people had come to help them move to Corhampton Road: Mr and Mrs Lester, Auntie Amy, John Watkins—anyone who had a car and a few hours to spare. Complete and utter chaos reigned in Newry Street, where Margaret sat in her wheelchair surrounded by her six-foot long drawing-board table, John's large desk, mattresses, baby equipment, suitcases, calipers and books.

'The new tenants will probably put just as much junk in again,' said John.

It showed just how wrong one can be. The young couple who were taking over the house had recently arrived back from a holiday in Sydney to find that their home in Warrandyte had been burnt to the ground in the devastating January bushfires. As soon as the Lesters had moved out of Newry Street with their carloads of impedimenta, the newcomers moved in with all they possessed —in one suitcase.

It was wonderful to have space to move about in and a pleasant garden to see from the windows. But as they settled into their new home it became evident that several alterations were needed if Margaret were to manage successfully on her own. Some were urgent. Others could wait until the couple were ready to spend the time and money involved. Gradually however the necessary modifications were made, and the result proved that the average home could be adapted very well for a disabled housewife, given a little thoughtful planning and not so very much money.

The first necessity was a ramp from the front door to the garden, without which Margaret would be completely housebound. Grandad Watkins took an enormous pride in helping John build this. He had long since retired after a distinguished career in electrical engineering, and he and Nonnie were delighted that Margaret and John were to live only a few miles away. He came often to suggest, alter or construct. Once or twice Nonnie Watkins came too, frail as a tiny bird, bringing a home-made cake in a basket on her arm.

144

David John

Margaret bathing Karen. Cindy helps by holding the powder tin, while visitor little Phil looks after the soap. (From the sleeve of the gramophone record 'Your New Baby', by courtesy W. & G. Record Processing Co. Pty Ltd, Melbourne)

Herald-Sun, Melbourne

Margaret Lester, Bachelor of Architecture, 4th March 1964

The other urgent task was to make bathroom, toilet and laundry accessible. As the toilet itself was wide enough for a wheelchair, it was only necessary to remove the door between it and the laundry and take off the bathroom door to give easy access.

That problem solved, Margaret turned her attention to the question of how to bath herself. She had decided to use the bath instead of the shower in the new house, but it was just too deep for her to manage easily. One day while trying to get out she had slipped—and there was no one in the house but herself and the baby. She had never felt safe with it since then. Nor did she approve of overhead showers for paraplegics. With so much of the body insensitive to heat and cold, it would be fatally easy to be scalded. After a great deal of thought she sketched a design for a bath seat that she thought might be successful, and took it to Mr Kingsmill, who was in charge of the Rehabilitation Workshop at the Austin Hospital. He examined it critically, said he thought it would work, and offered to let his boys construct it in the workshop if Margaret would pay for the timber.

John and Gerta were proudly ushered into the bathroom to see the result. It was a simple but ingenious wooden seat that fitted across the bath. It had a back for support, and underneath at each side was a piece of wood.

'The underneath bits stop it from slipping,' explained the designer.

'I see. And you shower yourself with this?'

Margaret had fixed a plastic hair hose to the hot and cold bath taps. John Watkins turned them on one at a time, controlling hot and cold until they combined into a warm spray.

'It works like a charm. Clever girl.'

'Wasn't it kind of Mr Kingsmill and the boys?'

'Yes, it was,' said Gerta. 'I'll bake them a big cake and Natalie shall take it over.' She did it the very next day.

The next enterprise was a little more complicated and expensive. The house had a back verandah that was going to be ideal for children to play on, particularly in wet weather. Meanwhile it was obviously the place for airing clothes, or sitting near the garden. Unfortunately it was on a different level from the rest of the house, which meant that there was a step down to it from both kitchen and laundry. Margaret and Cindy could not use it at all until the men built her a little ramp. She could then get from the kitchen to the verandah with the baby in her lap; but to go into the laundry to fetch clothes for airing she would have to shove the little ramp along with her wheelchair and manoeuvre it somehow into position, which was not easy. Nor was the ramp itself entirely satisfactory.

Grandad Watkins took this problem to heart. He pondered over it for weeks, pacing up and down, measuring and testing. At last one day he appeared triumphantly with a cheerful builder whom he introduced to John and Margaret.

'What are we going to build, Grandad?' Margaret asked, amused.

'Something we can afford, I hope,' said John, *sotto voce*.

Grandad overheard him. 'You don't have to build anything you don't want to. This is just a quote, see? I've been thinking a lot about that back verandah. I'd like to see you get rid of that little ramp. Throw it away. What you need is a floor on the same level as the rest of the house, a wooden one. If you can afford to get one built I'll—I'll give it a plastic coating for you.'

The Lesters thought it a wonderful idea, which it was. It was not unduly expensive; the project when completed meant that Margaret had access to a splendid covered outdoor area; in effect, also, she could wheel her chair with ease from one end of the house to the other. It meant too that a baby could be pushed out in the moses basket for fresh air or a sunbath.

The next area they tackled was the laundry. They had bought an old washing-machine together with the house, but with young children there would always be a need for troughs for soaking and rinsing, as well as for general household purposes, and those in the laundry were far too high. A plumber was called in to lower them to a suitable wheelchair height. This left only one major problem in connection with the laundry: it was still impossible for Margaret to get into the back garden to peg out the clothes.

The family discussed it over coffee.

'Could we dig up the rotary clothes line and jam it against the back verandah?' asked someone.

'What about when it swings around and cracks someone on the head?'

'Me, for instance,' said Margaret.

'Don't worry, twit,' said her husband, patting her on the head. 'This wood's hard enough to stand anything.'

146

'It would be a big job, and it wouldn't look very nice,' objected Margaret, making a face at him. 'I think we'll just have to build another ramp. A big one, on legs, like a sort of bridge from the verandah to ground level. I can peg out the clothes from the ramp itself or use it to get down into the backyard. It'll have to be fairly long, or the grade will be too steep for me to wheel up from the garden.'

'The one we built at Ryeburne Avenue would have been just perfect,' said John Watkins, regretfully. 'I say!' he exclaimed suddenly. 'I've an idea. I don't know whether it will work—it all depends on whether they're using it or not.'

'What on earth are you talking about, Dad?'

'The ramp at Ryeburne Avenue! If they're not using it they might sell it back to us.'

It was such a typical Watkins idea that everybody burst out laughing.

'But I'm perfectly serious! Tell you what, if they'll sell it, I'll pay for it and give it to you young people as a gift.'

'I'll go halves on that,' Grandad put in swiftly.

'Done.'

'Hey, wait a minute—what about transporting it from Ryeburne Avenue?'

'I'll go halves on that too,' said Grandad. 'Chop it in half. John, you bring your half on the roof of your car. I'll bring my half on mine.'

In due course the dismembering took place, but the ramp, like Gaul, had to be divided into three parts. Grandad took the smallest portion, and headed for Corhampton Road. He was so excited that he shot into the carport completely forgetting the load tied on the roof of his car. Crunch! The awful sounds which rent the air proceeded from the driver as well as the load; they brought Margaret racing down the front ramp in her wheelchair.

The other two parts were transported by John Watkins and Natalie's husband Cliff.

But the various parts were still very far from being united. Post-holes had to be dug. John Watkins had an accumulation of work, and was off overseas again. Cliff was busy. Grandad was rapidly beginning to age and could do less and less. The big wooden sections lay neglected in the back garden for months until in desperation Margaret persuaded Ian to help. He came several times after lectures to dig the post-holes. When all was ready he organized the men of the family and together with a student friend they hoisted the ramp into position and made all secure.

'Hooray!' cried Margaret. 'Thank you all!' Triumphantly she sailed out from the verandah, pegged a bib on the clothes hoist, and whizzed on down into the garden. Later John Watkins made a balustrade from a length of solid waterpipe; the clothes hoist 'flying bridge' was now completely safe.

One more adaptation remained to make a satisfactory wheelchair house. The Lesters had been in Corhampton Road nearly four years when Margaret at last achieved the ambition of every wheelchair wife—a wheelchair sink. Formerly she had had to do her washing-up sideways to the sink, which was built for a standing adult and was therefore too high. As soon as they could spare the money they engaged a plumber and carpenter to alter the kitchen. Cupboards were made more convenient. The one under the sink was removed altogether and the sink lowered. The bottom was covered with asbestos cement and the pipe well lagged so that the metal could not burn her unfeeling legs. Now she could wheel in frontways with her knees under the sink and do the dishes in comfort.

'It's wonderful. Really, there's nothing I would rather have had,' she said to John, looking around their home with great satisfaction and pride. A few chores had sometimes to be left undone, but on the whole it was as comfortable and well-run as that of any young woman on two strong legs.

thirteen || WHEELCHAIR ARCHITECT

'What are you going to do about your degree?' Ann Pennington had kept needling Margaret, during the period when the Austin Spinal Centre team was still training her to cope with life in a wheelchair.

'I suppose I'll settle down and finish it some time,' was the reply.

'Fine. Then why not now? What is it you still have to do? Design Five? What does that involve?'

'A thesis, for one thing, with a special design of my own, and a written report, and various designs on set subjects.'

'Well you could do some of it here in hospital, couldn't you?'

'I suppose so, but I'd need a drawing-board.'

'With all those engineers in your family, couldn't someone rig you up one?'

'I guess so,' said Margaret.

The family engineers thoroughly approved of the idea. John Watkins set up two sloping supports for the drawing-board, on the bench on the hospital verandah; Natalie brought in textbooks and drawing materials. Margaret sat at the improvised drawing-board, surrounded by work, and dreamed of her future marriage.

For when it actually came to the point, the same thing happened as before—the cogwheels of her mind seemed to jam. The old drive and concentration had gone. It seemed far more important to concentrate on delightful plans for the wedding, and her future with John.

Her interest in architectural studies was not really rekindled until the following year when she was tutoring at the university.

'If you can tutor then you can jolly well finish your degree,' said John Lester, who was himself studying part-time for his Arts degree. 'You're nutty not to do it while you have the chance— you'll regret it all your life.'

Gerta and John were of the same opinion. 'You never know when you might be glad to have that degree,' said Gerta. 'Life is so unexpected. Suppose you want to take up professional work some time in the future. There might be a job you particularly wanted to do. Wouldn't you be mad if you couldn't because you'd just missed out on the necessary qualifications.'

The university also gave Margaret every encouragement.

One morning she was tidying up the little Carlton house when the phone rang. It was Professor Brian Lewis from the university.

'Have you heard about our new drawing-board for disabled students?' he asked her.

'No!' She was interested at once.

'We saw it when we went to Japan recently.'

'With the students?'

'Yes. It's a mechanical drawing-table and drawing machine made by Mutoh Drafter Industries in Tokyo. They're giving one to Melbourne University as a goodwill gesture. I thought you might be interested.'

'I certainly am! I have great difficulty trying to use an ordinary drawing-board from my wheelchair.'

'I think you'd be delighted with this one. We'd be very happy for you to use it while you are completing your degree. Are you doing anything this evening? Would you like to come and demonstrate it for us? It's to be presented tonight by the Japanese Consul-General. Could John bring you?'

'John's got lectures tonight, and Dad's overseas, but my mother might like to come with me.'

'Good, then we'll expect you.'

'Darling, of course I will. It will be fun!' exclaimed Gerta at once, when she heard about the drawing-board. But neither she nor Margaret was prepared for the barrage of reporters and photographers who were waiting at the university.

'Heavens, just as well I wore my velvet coat,' whispered Margaret. 'Do I look seven months pregnant?'

'Yes, darling, and you should be proud of it,' replied Gerta. 'So don't worry.'

Margaret had no time to worry, for she was immediately greeted by Professor Lewis and introduced to Mr Katashi Suga, the Japanese Consul-General, and Mr Zwarteveen, the agent for Mutoh Drafter Industries, the firm which had manufactured the equipment and were now presenting it to the university.

Mr Zwarteveen showed her its special features.

'These pedals, you see, raise and lower the board. They can be worked by either hands or feet. The stand can be rotated and inclined to eight-five degrees. Perhaps you would like to try it yourself?'

Margaret wheeled herself up to the board and tried it out.

'It's wonderful,' she said. 'I can adjust it to whatever height or angle I like, and I don't have to stretch at all.'

Mr Zwarteveen bowed.

'I hope the board will be of some help to you in gaining your degree in Architecture, Mrs Lester.'

They had what Margaret told John was a fantastic supper, and she went home determined to resume her studies.

Within a few weeks came doctors' orders to retire to bed for a month before her baby was born. Cindy's birth and the joys and responsibilities of new motherhood were followed immediately by the upheaval of settling into the home at North Balwyn. But one day in March 1962 she went to the university, and with Cindy in her arms, resolutely enrolled for Design Part Five.

'It's now or never,' she said when she came home and told John what she had done.

'Good, but where are the lectures being held?' he asked instantly. They both knew that Melbourne University was crammed to overflowing.

'It's that burnt-out taxi building in Swanston Street,' she said. 'They've rented the upstairs.'

'I know that building,' he groaned. 'It has a hideous flight of stairs. Have you seen them?'

'Yes.'

'Well?'

'I'm not going to give up just because of a flight of stairs. We'll have to work something out. Marion is going to help me.' John's sister Marion, who had been Margaret's bridesmaid, was now in her final year of architecture at Melbourne University.

'Some of the work to be done is sketch designing—that is, sketching a subject without preparation. Mr Berg, the lecturer, says he'll ring me up and tell me the subject on the day and I can do it at home. And he'll drop in and help me occasionally, when he can, on the major subjects.'

'That's good of him. What about Cindy?'

'Nat says she'll baby-sit when necessary. I'll have to go in sometimes for criticism—you know, they pin up all the designs and criticize them in front of the whole group. Someone will have to carry me upstairs on those days.'

Margaret plunged into her architectural studies with her usual determination. It was inevitable that from time to time she would have to spend weeks in bed because of 'skin-off'. Arrangements would have to be made for the baby, and the designs she had to complete would be put aside. She struggled on, however, and managed to pass all the design subjects.

'Only your thesis now,' encouraged Gerta. 'Let me have Cindy for a few weeks, while you settle down and complete it.'

The idea for the thesis, an original design without which she could not complete her degree, had lain at the back of Margaret's mind for several years. One of the requirements was that it be planned for an actual site. Margaret had decided on a natural-history museum, as she considered that the surroundings of Melbourne's existing museum, in the heart of the city, were too dingy. During her preliminary research she discovered that six and a half acres of parkland had actually been reserved by the government for such a purpose. On visiting the site she found it inspiring. The land was an irregular, interesting shape, with many well-grown trees; it was in close proximity to Melbourne's Shrine of Remembrance and to the beautiful botanic gardens, with good transport to city and suburbs. She went to the Lands Department and bought an aerial photograph of the site and maps of the district. Slowly the idea of the museum took shape in her mind. Through all the months of her engagement, the long period in hospital, the first years of marriage and motherhood, it kept returning, each time with a new section or another addition to the plans. Sometimes she jotted down desultory sketches or notes; she knew however that the idea could never come to fruition until at some stage she could concentrate all her energies on it to the exclusion of everything else. Cindy was at the mischievous running-around stage. Impossible to concentrate when she was in the house. She decided to accept Gerta's offer.

With the house quiet she took out her working materials and tried her best—but once again she bogged down. It was the time factor that defeated her. Cindy returned home. The thesis was still incomplete. She felt it would never be otherwise.

And then in June 1963 came another major interruption, in the person of baby Karen. Her studies were once more swamped in the joys and responsibilities of motherhood. It was some time before she even remembered her thesis. But one day, while hunting through her desk for a letter she had lost, she came across a sheaf of notes about her museum. John came home late to find her sitting at her desk reading them, and trying to feed Karen at the same time. Cindy had crept out of bed and was crouched behind the wheelchair with a toy, hoping not to be noticed.

'How's it going?' he asked.

'I'm just realizing that it's no use,' said Margaret, pushing the papers aside. 'I'm giving it away.'

'Now, don't be silly—'

'Well, it's impossible. Till the children grow up, anyway.'

'I'll get you a mothercraft nurse for four weeks if you'll promise to sit at your drawing-board until you finish it.'

'We can't afford it!'

'I know we can't. But we'll do it. Put an ad. in the paper tomorrow. Now, where's the quietest place for the drawing-board? Out of the reach of the kids!'

The next day they advertised for a mothercraft nurse and were lucky enough to get one.

The Japanese drawing-board was set up in their bedroom near the window, and there Margaret sat every day for a month, wrestling with her natural-history museum.

Karina and Jim Webb, two architect friends, came the first week

153

and perched on the bed to give advice and criticism. She badly needed their encouragement, for she still secretly doubted her own ability. Then, suddenly and unbelievably, the whole project began to gather momentum. Freed from her constant absorption in the food, clothes and hygiene of the two children, Margaret began to dream about anthropology and ethnology, palaeontology and zoology. The second week, however, just as things were going swimmingly, she began to panic about air-conditioning.

'What if it's not right! I don't *know* enough about the mechanical side of it,' she wailed, slamming shut a most unhelpful book on the subject.

'Then consult someone who does, instead of getting in a twit,' was John's calm suggestion. 'Surely we know enough mechanical engineers.'

'Maureen Mackie's husband, Peter!'

'Naturally.'

Peter Georgeson amiably sorted out her air-conditioning worries. The design was now approaching completion, and the family was beginning to get excited about it.

'It's a pity it can't actually be built,' said Natalie, who had dropped in to admire and encourage. 'Is it really as near completion as it looks?'

'Well, I think so. But it depends on whether all the structural part is correct. Bruce Miller has promised to come out and check it thoroughly with me—he's a civil engineer.'

'Can I come in?' asked a wistful little voice from the doorway.

'Come and give Mummy a big hug,' said Margaret warmly. 'Look, Mummy's drawings are nearly finished, and soon I won't be a busy old Mummy any more, and we'll have lots of fun together.'

Two weeks later she flung her pencil on the floor and whipped her wheelchair into the kitchen where Cindy and the baby were being fed.

'I've done it!' she exclaimed. 'I've done it! Come and give Mummy a hug, Cindy.' If she could have danced for joy she would have done so. 'The relief—I just can't believe it.'

John grinned. 'I knew you could do it.'

'I've just had an awful thought. What if they don't accept it!'

'So what? You'll just have to do it again.'

'Don't,' she groaned.

'Come on, you hobo, what you need is a nice strong cup of coffee. So, how about making me one?'

'Well, really—'

'Too proud, now that you're about to graduate? All right, I'll make it this once.'

'Suppose they don't pass it. Suppose I don't hear?'

'You'll hear.'

They heard four days before Christmas.

Margaret graduated on 4th March 1964.

'I wish you could be there, Mum,' she said as she sat by Gerta's bedside on the eve of the great day. Gerta had been desperately ill; in the Box Hill Hospital she was slowly fighting her way back to precarious life.

'Darling, you don't know how happy I am. You already have John and your two dear little girls. And now you've completed your professional training—' Her voice faltered a little. She was so very anxious that each of her children should be well-prepared for the time when they must continue without her guidance and protection, for she knew her years were numbered. Every achievement of Margaret's was doubly significant, for it proved that despite her physical disabilities, her spirit was undaunted. As long as this was so, Gerta knew she could cope with her unresponsive body.

Melbourne University degrees were traditionally conferred at Wilson Hall in the university grounds.

'More steps to the platform,' said John resignedly. 'I suppose your father and I will have to carry you up in the chair to receive your degree. Everyone will be able to have a good look at your new shoes, anyway.'

Margaret laughed, burying her face in the flowers Gerta had sent. The new black shoes to go with her cap and gown had been bought on one of their hurried shopping expeditions into the city. Gerta had sent the money as a graduation present.

'They look very nice,' said Mrs Lester senior. They were all waiting, with John Watkins and Natalie (now Mrs Bills) in the foyer of the hall, which was crammed with excited graduates and their friends. Some undergraduate ushers seized Margaret's chair.

'You're to go on the platform,' they said.

'Oh *no!*'

'Sure. With all the bigwigs. Then you just wheel forward when your name is called. Is that all right?'

'I suppose so,' she laughed. 'I'll have to try to look inconspicuous.'

She was bowled down the aisle and hoisted on to the platform, where she sat, very conspicuously indeed, near Douglas Annand's great mural of man striving upwards to the light out of primeval slime. The organ music began, and down the aisle came the Chancellor and his party in their colourful hoods and gowns, followed by the graduates. The official party filed on to the platform and the ceremony commenced. It seemed hours before the architecture graduates were presented; then at last, 'Margaret Anne Lester', called the impersonal voice. She wheeled herself forward, received her degree, and retired to her place.

When it was over she had to wait until willing hands lifted her chair down from the platform into the body of the hall. Only then was she free, like all the other graduates, to rejoin family and friends, and receive their congratulations.

'We're proud of you,' said John Watkins when, having fought their way through the crowd, they surrounded her chair. John Lester said little; he merely beamed as he stood close by her side.

'John's going to be the next,' said Margaret happily.

'We hope,' he said.

'We'll look forward to it,' said John Watkins. 'When will it be?'

'Next March, I hope—that is, if—'

'Of course you will,' said Margaret. 'If I can do it, so can you.' They smiled at each other. It had not been easy for either of them, but it was worth it.

Twelve months later, in the same hall, the position was reversed. Margaret sat proudly in the body of Wilson Hall while John received the degree of Bachelor of Arts.

fourteen || WHEELCHAIR MERMAID

Occupied first with her marriage and then with the advent of Cindy, Margaret had for a time completely forgotten about sport, until one day she heard in conversation that her friend Jess Menzies, the mother of five children, went swimming regularly at the Box Hill Squash Bowl.

'Wouldn't I love that!' she exclaimed.

'Well, why don't you come too?' asked Jess. 'I go every week with Helann Rowland—she has four children. It's only a few miles from where you live.'

Margaret hesitated. 'I seem to remember a lot of steps at that pool, and aren't the toilets rather narrow?'

'Oh, we'll help you. Don't worry. Shall we pick you up?'

'No thank you, I can get there on my own.'

Jess and Helann appointed themselves Margaret's unofficial trainers and with regular practice her backstroke soon became quite powerful.

Meanwhile, paraplegic sport had been developing fast at the Austin Spinal Centre. This aspect of rehabilitation was now under the charge of a diplomate in Physical Education, Eva Zselenyi, working as assistant to Mr Sanderson, the Head Remedial

157

Gymnast. Like the rest of the staff, she was devoted to her patients' interests. More of them were now becoming interested in swimming, and since there was still no pool at the Austin, she accompanied them on weekly trips to the Box Hill Pool, where those who most needed hydrotherapy could receive this valuable treatment. Transport was arranged by the Donvale Ladies' Auxiliary of the Paraplegic Association, under the direction of Mrs Cheshire. Margaret was invited to join in these sessions too. Before long her name was being considered as a possible competitor for the Third Australian Paraplegic Games to be held in Adelaide in 1964.

'But I can only do backstroke!' she exclaimed.

'Well, you'll just have to learn breaststroke.'

Afraid though she was, she turned on to her front. Thanks to the same dogged determination she brought to most of her undertakings, it was not long before she was able to swim breaststroke. Once she had mastered it she tackled freestyle as well; her fears vanished and she now felt quite comfortable in the water.

All competitors in the Paraplegic Sports had to be members of the Paraplegic Association which had its own sports club and published its own magazine, called *Paravics*. Margaret had been a member of the Association since hospital days when Gerta had come dashing into the ward one day to tell her that Dr Cheshire's secretary, Miss Winter, was a paraplegic.

Margaret was suitably impressed. The only other paraplegic she had yet known to be in full-time employment was Helen Gillies.

'She must be good if Dr Cheshire employs her. As a matter of fact, I want to meet her anyway. Dr Cheshire suggests that I join the Paraplegic Association—he says Miss Winter will tell me all about it and fix it for me. She's on the committee.'

'Do you think that's a good idea?' asked Gerta doubtfully. 'Wouldn't you be happier in your own circle of able-bodied people instead of having everybody around you in wheelchairs?'

'I don't think it would be like that at all. We've got to have an association to work for the good of all of us paraplegics. I guess I should be a member. I might be able to help in some way. Maybe with my architectural training.'

Gerta was silent, repressing the pain of the phrase 'us paraplegics'.

Eventually Margaret had her talk with Miss Winter, and subsequently the Association gained several new members, for Gerta, John Watkins and Grandad Watkins all decided to pay membership fees too.

As a member of Paravics Margaret made many friends, and received a great deal of encouragement in her sporting activities.

At Mentone she was generously helped by Mr Timmermans, the Paraplegic Sports Club's swimming coach, who gave endless time to helping paraplegics. He and his wife Claire had opened a heated indoor swimming pool called the Swimwell Pool, and at scheduled times this was made freely available to the disabled people in training. It was largely owing to the efforts of 'Tim and Claire' that Victoria was regarded as a formidable competitor in interstate paraplegic swimming events.

Mr Sanderson heard about Margaret's swimming and told her she should do other sports besides swimming if she wished to be considered for the Adelaide Games. He suggested javelin throwing, discus throwing and putting the shot, and invited her to practise regularly at the Austin with the other patients. Margaret accepted with enthusiasm. She found that hurling the discus was tremendous fun, and good for letting off steam. Taking her turn with the boys, she soon became quite adept. The shotput required more effort. But javelin throwing was the most difficult. There were two types: distance throwing and precision throwing, both imposing the same physical strains as archery.

'I can't balance my body when I throw,' she complained to Mr Sanderson. Dr Cheshire would have told her that that was precisely why the sport was prescribed for paraplegics.

Mr Sanderson said that she needed more practice, and lent her a javelin and a discus to take home. John painted a target for her on the short grass in the back garden. He was horrified when he returned home next evening, to hear Margaret calling, 'Fetch it, Cindy! Fetch it for Mummy!'

He came out on to the back verandah to see Cindy's plump little legs twinkling across the garden as she rushed to retrieve the long, pointed javelin, which, he scarcely noticed, was remarkably close to the target.

'She'll kill herself,' he expostulated. 'You shouldn't let her do it.'

'But she stands well out of the way while I throw. How can she come to any harm just fetching it?'

'She could fall on to the point that's sticking out of the ground.'

'Don't worry,' Margaret reassured him, 'she's got too much sense.'

They watched the child tug the seven-foot long javelin out of the ground and stagger back with it to her mother.

'Good girl,' said Margaret, while Cindy flung herself on to her father and kissed him.

John shook his head. He preferred it when Margaret played table-tennis on the family table-tennis board which her father had set up in the garage. Judy Cook, a friend from university days, and Pam McCarthy, a fellow member of Paravics, came regularly to practise with her.

With her usual determination Margaret worked regularly until the time came for the team to be chosen. Gerta, although now very frail, insisted on coming to both field and swimming trials. She saw every one of the performances that without a doubt qualified Margaret to represent her State in Adelaide. Moving slowly with her four-point stick, she came up to the wheelchair, her face shining, and told Margaret she was proud of her.

Most of the Victorian paraplegic team were driving the five hundred miles to Adelaide. Margaret decided to fly, and since it was school holidays Jo would go with her. The two sisters had never been away together before and were delighted, for there was a deep affection between them.

A young paraplegic from Hobart, Angus Downie, was on the same plane. When they reached Adelaide he and Margaret were put into their wheelchairs and lowered to the ground by forklift. It was slightly nerve-racking, but at least it was better than being carried, Margaret thought.

Relatives were waiting to greet them and to drive Jo to the Morris Hospital where the interstate paraplegics were to be accommodated. Margaret went with the other sports competitors in the big bus which was fitted with a hydraulic lift for disabled people. They met again at the hospital, now the scene of much activity. Competitors in chairs from various States, smart in their neat blazers with badges, wheeled excitedly to and fro, renewing friendships from previous interstate meetings. Mr Thomas, Fred

160

Martin, Tim Timmermans, Eva Zselenyi and Mr Luke worked like beavers as they took care of the arrangements for the Victorian team. Margaret saw Elaine Schreiber and Bruno Moretti talking to Alan Robertson and several other fellow members. The babel of voices was almost deafening, and there was a general air of festivity. Margaret was reminded vividly of the days when she lay in the Acute Ward and watched the antics of visiting wheelchair athletes in her reflector mirror.

'People often say it's as well we can't see into the future, but sometimes it would be encouraging,' she thought. 'I had no idea then that four years later I'd be in a team myself, awaiting the arrival of my husband and children. I'm so lucky.'

John Lester could only take one day off work. He was to pick up Cindy and baby Karen from Mrs Lester senior in Blackburn on Thursday evening, drive 186 miles to Horsham, stay at a motel and continue on to Adelaide in time to see Margaret compete in the Games.

Thursday evening in Melbourne was cold and foggy. Mrs Lester longed to put Cindy and Karen into warm beds instead of into a car for a long journey interstate. She watched as John fished in his pockets for a long ribbon of paper, to make a final check of the list of necessities Margaret had told him to bring. Both he and Margaret had long mustard-coloured windcheaters with hoods that drooped across the back. John's came about to his knees, and had an enormous pocket across the stomach. He had a habit of tucking both hands into it, giving a fleeting impression of a tall kangaroo with its jocy in its pouch.

'Portable ice-box, fruit juices, disposable nappies, plastic bags, tinned milk, bottles, bottle-tea-cosy, cheese, fruit, dry biscuits, rugs, Karen's teddy, Cindy's teddy, clean pants, slippers, plastic jugs, jackets, coats, car-seats, pusher, toothbrushes, washers, towels, tin-opener—and see that they spend a penny before they get into the car.'

Mr Lester came out to see them off. Cindy was strapped into the car-seat beside her father. Karen was securely fastened in hers in the back. Each little girl was dressed in bright warm overalls and a warm sweater; each hugged a teddy bear. Around them were packed all the articles on John's list and a dozen more. Scarcely a cubic inch remained unoccupied. Cindy's eyes were as round as saucers. She was anxious to 'go to Adelaide to see

Mummy', but she had never seen fog before, and was more than a little apprehensive. But she waved cheerfully to her grandparents as the car went forward down the drive and swung off into the foggy darkness.

For the first fifty miles of the trip the fog compelled John to drive so slowly that he dropped well behind schedule. Karen had fallen asleep bolt upright, like a little Indian baby on its mother's back; Cindy, relieved when the fog gave way to clear darkness, was fascinated by tiny diamonds that began to sparkle on the windscreen.

'Look, pretty,' she said leaning forward and stretching out her hand.

'Sit still—good girl,' said John absently. He was taking advantage of the clearing of the fog to increase his speed—he could see that now a rainstorm was coming up and that very soon visibility would be almost as bad again.

Cindy gave a little sigh. 'Where's Mummy?' she asked.

'Mummy's in Adelaide,' explained John patiently. 'Soon we'll come to a nice house and have a lovely sleep. Then we'll see Mummy tomorrow.' The rain was lashing the windscreen now, dancing greyly in the headlight beams, swishing under the tyres. Cindy's eyelids fluttered and closed. She slept suddenly, teddy still clasped to her chest.

The car suddenly began to swerve and pull out of John's control. He slowed to a standstill and, fishing for a torch, groped his way out into the pouring rain. It was as he thought: a tyre had burst. He said a bad word under his breath and began to prepare to change the wheel by torchlight in the driving rain. As he opened the door to search for some tools, a huge transport came racing towards them. With its glaring headlights and its enormous bulk outlined in red lights, it rattled past like something in a nightmare. To make matters worse, it carried a cargo of lowing cattle; the driver, seeing a man getting out of a stationary car, sounded his horn as a warning. The shattering noise jerked both infants awake; they screamed with terror. John soothed and petted them; but no sooner would he have them quiet than another transport would loom frighteningly out of the rain, for they were on the main highway between Melbourne and Adelaide and the traffic was heavy. What with reassuring the children and changing the wheel, it was after midnight when they finally drove into the darkened township of Horsham and found their way to the motel. They were all exhausted.

Hunger and other needs woke the children next morning. John crawled out of bed, tired as he still was. The two infants had to be washed, dressed and fed, the tyre must be mended so that he would have a spare one for the road in case the same thing happened again, and he still had several hundred miles to go. He'd long since given up hope of reaching Adelaide in time to see Margaret take part in the javelin, discus and club throwing that afternoon; he was determined however to see her compete in the swimming events which began at seven-thirty that evening.

It was several hours before they were on their way again; then the same thing happened—a flat tyre.

Congratulating himself on having had the other one repaired, he set to work once more to change the wheel. This time, cold and raining though it still was, he could at least see what he was doing. The children watched with interest, their noses glued against the car windows, longing to get out so they could have a better view.

'You're a pair of grubs,' said John fondly, wiping both noses and windows with a handful of tissues. For the umpteenth time he fed them, toileted Cindy, poured her some fruit juice from a tin, changed Karen's pants and gave her a drink of warm milk from her bottle in the special warmer. He was determined to give them neither food nor drink that he had not prepared with his own hands—they had to be delivered to their mother free of any possible wogs. Baby Karen rewarded him with a wide smile. He settled them into their car-seats and took to the road again. It stretched before him endlessly black, wet and shiny, like some kind of hypnotic device. To his dismay he found himself nodding at the wheel, with still a hundred miles to go. The long drive and the lack of sufficient sleep were catching up on him. He pulled up at the side of the road and lifted Cindy into back of the car.

'Daddy's going to have a sleep,' he said. 'You two little girls just sit there and have a play with your teddies.'

They looked at him solemnly. Cindy's lip began to quiver.

'Good girls,' he added hopefully. His eyes closed of their own accord, but his brain remained alert to every slightest move of the children. They were obedient little girls, but who could ever

163

be sure of what a child might do next? The traffic was heavy, the car doors were locked, but an agile little girl might perhaps unwind a window and climb out.

He stretched out a long arm towards their fat little knees. Karen's damp fist closed around his forefinger, but he heard Cindy give a tiny sigh and begin to whisper to her teddy.

Margaret had won several silver medals in field events that afternoon, but she hoped to do still better in the swimming, which was to be held at the Unley Pool at Forestville. She was looking forward to a tussle with Lorraine Dodd, a Western Australian who had a fantastic record as a paraplegic sportswoman and held the world record in A Grade for backstroke. It was a great disappointment when one of paraplegia's common ills put Lorraine out of action, leaving Margaret the only competitor in her swimming events. It took the edge off her excitement, which was dimmed further by the intense cold and her worry over John and the children, who still had not arrived. It was a bitter evening; in the tent that had been erected near the water the competitors were being constantly rubbed with liniment under carefully controlled oil heaters.

Margaret's anxiety increased as the swimming events began and still John had not appeared. But just as she was being lifted from the water after her second race, she suddenly saw his familiar tall figure strolling along the concourse. The baby was in the pusher; Cindy was trotting alongside, clutching her teddy. It only needed a glance for Margaret to see that the children were clean, neat and happy. The only sign of their journey was that Cindy was wearing her bedroom slippers. A shoe had been mislaid en route.

As she began the 25 metres backstroke race, her enormous relief suddenly gave her an extra surge of power.

'I'll jolly well swim as if Lorraine *is* here,' she told herself. She shot off, arms threshing the water like propellers. She had never swum so well.

The Australian spectators, many of them disabled, responded instantly to the spectacle of a competitor straining to give the best performance of which she was capable, irrespective of whether or not there was anyone to beat. They cheered her on till they were hoarse.

She heard the shouting dimly through the splashing of the water;

suddenly her hands touched the edge of the pool. Someone lifted her out of the water, and Dr Cheshire was there, grasping her shoulder in excitement and exclaiming, 'Margaret, you've done it in thirty-four point nine seconds. You've equalled the world record! Well done!'

That night she gained three gold medals for swimming.

Two years later when the Australian Paraplegic Games were held in Brisbane, Margaret was again in the Victorian team. This time she won so many medals—for swimming, shotput, table-tennis, discus, club-throwing and wheelchair race, that she lost count, and couldn't remember whether it was ten or eleven. It was not important, because for Margaret, as for all the other disabled people who take part in sport, the game itself was enough.

For those disabled people who are successfully rehabilitated have a special task to perform. It is true that they find in sport a physical and emotional satisfaction that makes an enormous contribution to their own health and well-being. But by taking part in the community effort of organized interstate and international games, they also demonstrate to the world that a handicapped person is not someone to be put aside, pensioned off, or utterly forgotten: he is a human being with the same desires, needs and rights as anyone else. He has brothers and sisters all over the world. Given a chance, he can prove over and over again that, being disabled, a person yet has ability.

It rained next day, as it had done for practically the whole of the Adelaide Paraplegic Games. But nothing could dampen the enthusiasm of the Lester family. John insisted on remaining in charge of the children, with Jo's able assistance. Margaret, he said, was on holiday, and was not to do a thing. With John wheeling the pusher, they splashed around watching the wheelchair archery, table-tennis, and basketball played on a waterlogged court. After a community picnic lunch on a verandah they said goodbye to their team-mates. Victoria had done well, coming second to New South Wales and winning sixteen gold medals, three of which were Margaret's swimming medals. Two Victorians, Elaine Schreiber and Michael Daw, had been chosen to represent Australia in the team which was to compete at the International Stoke Mandeville Games in Tokyo.

Somehow John achieved the impossible, cramming everyone

165

and their belongings into the car. They drove the five hundred miles in high spirits, stopping at Mt Lofty for a leisurely visit to friends and spending a night at a motel. They arrived back on the Sunday night, tired but happy.

The children rushed into the house to find the toys they had had to leave behind.

'This is where you take over again, honeybun,' said John contentedly.

fifteen || A SON IS BORN

Margaret was feeling strangely unwell.

The year had started badly with what should have been a carefree seaside holiday at Merricks, but, for her at least, was one long-drawn-out irritation. The house they were in, while fairly convenient for someone chairborne, was in such a position that it was very difficult for her to get to the beach. The rough tracks and dry sand were almost impassable for a wheelchair. So while John took the two little girls to the beach every day, she stayed in the house, rapidly becoming hotter and crosser.

One day they drove to Shoreham, a smooth sandy beach that they thought it might be possible to negotiate. The children scrambled out of the car and Margaret looked eagerly towards the water, cool and inviting, such a short distance away. She began to turn the wheels of her chair. In a few seconds they were bogged down in the loose sand. John swung the chair round, tipped it up on its back wheels, and tugged, tossing his head to keep his dark hair out of his eyes.

'Get off, Cindy! Look, you and Karen run down and have a paddle. Mummy and I are coming.'

Too independent to look about him for assistance, he pulled

and struggled until with arms nearly wrenched from their sockets he had her at the water's edge. There, much as he disliked doing so, he was forced to accept help. A young man in a swimsuit helped him lift Margaret out of the chair, they waded out until the water was deep enough to float, and plopped her in.

'Mummy's swimming!' laughed the little girls. They splashed about while Margaret thankfully floated along until she felt the familiar wonderful buoyancy of deeper water supporting her—then away she swam with long, powerful strokes. It was not just a question of coolness on a hot summer's day. No one but a paraplegic could understand the joy of regaining that swift, independent motion that could now only be hers when she was swimming or driving a car.

When at last she swam back to shore, greatly refreshed, the young man appeared again and helped John lift her into her wheelchair and back over the sand to the car. It was the only bright spot of the holiday.

Somehow she did not manage any more swimming that holiday. The time dragged on. While the rest of the family became brown and fit she became paler and grumpier than ever. It was a relief when the holiday was over and she was able to resume her familiar routine back at home. The change had done her no good; in fact she felt so unwell that there was nothing for it but a return visit to the Austin to find out what was wrong. Probably an infection so common to her disability. Mrs Lester came to baby-sit and Margaret set off. Always before, when anything was wrong, Gerta had accompanied her, but now she was too unwell herself. For the first time Margaret was going alone. She felt sick and depressed.

The doctor finished his examination and regarded his patient, who was lying on the bed in the familiar surroundings of Ward Eighteen.

'I'm not sure exactly what this is, but perhaps you could tell me—do you think it is possible that you might be having another baby?'

Margaret's face lit up. 'Yes, it could be that.'

'Well, we'd better find out. We'll get some tests made. Because if it's not that we've got to find out what's wrong.'

It seemed an eternity of days before the results of the tests were through, and then one day came a phone call from the hospital.

168

'Margaret, we've had the report of those tests.'

'Yes?' Margaret waited breathlessly.

'They're negative. I'm sorry you're disappointed—but look, I'm not satisfied. These tests are not always a hundred per cent reliable. I'd like you to go along to the Women's Hospital and have Professor Townsend examine you. It's important that we know one way or the other.'

This time Margaret had to drive herself into the city. The traffic was heavier than ever and as usual there was not a parking space in sight. 'Well, I've *got* to see the doctor—it's just too bad,' she said in exasperation, pulling up fair and square in the middle of a 'No Parking' sign painted on the road. She piloted her chair through the streams of cars, ignoring the surprised glances of drivers and hoping that she was conspicuous enough not to be clocked.

A young girl was coming out of the hospital entrance holding on to her mother's arm. Their shining faces told the story even before the two nurses appeared behind them, each carrying a small white bundle.

'Twins!' thought Margaret happily. 'Maybe that's a good omen.'

Once again the waiting, the careful examination, the suspense. She waited quietly. A new baby with all its joys and responsibilities, or another of those illnesses that are the bane of the paraplegic's life: probably hospitalization, weeks in bed, the whole dreary routine . . . ?

'Yes,' said the doctor. 'No doubt about it.' He did some swift calculations. 'End of August, I should say. Are you glad?'

'I should say so! We'd always planned to have a big family.'

'Three's a big enough family for you,' said the doctor firmly. 'This has got to be the last, Margaret. You've been very lucky so far, no complications, but it's silly to tempt fate. You would be very foolish to have more. I certainly wouldn't advise it.'

'Well, if I can't have any more we'll adopt one.'

'Are you serious?'

'Of course.'

The doctor shook his head. 'I think you've got just about enough to cope with. Four might be one too many. Besides, I doubt if you'd get one to adopt. So many couples are waiting who have no children at all. They'd have first preference. Anyway, let's concentrate on this one.'

Outside the hospital the city traffic flowed on as relentlessly as ever. Looking across to her car Margaret suddenly saw a man in uniform leaning purposefully against the bonnet, pencil and notebook in hand.

'The beast! He's waiting to book me!' she thought, recollecting the 'No Parking' sign. She trundled across the road. The man's glance fell on her and Margaret was amused to see his expression change as she approached her car. He sprang up, tucking the notebook into his pocket.

'Can I help you?'

Margaret smiled. Producing her keys she let him open the car door. She heaved herself into the car, and let him fold the heavy chair and stow it beside her.

'That's a wonderful help,' she said graciously. 'I have to be careful—you see I'm going to have a baby.'

Natalie was surprised that her sister showed no outward excitement over the coming of her third child.

'I'll rejoice when the baby is safely here,' Margaret said quietly. She knew now exactly what was involved. Every year brought the inevitable times when she had to lie in bed, sometimes for weeks on end, until some skin-break healed. Pregnancy added other complications, plus the inescapable month in bed before the baby was born. Every time that she was out of action brought the problem of who would look after the rest of the family. Occasionally she was lucky enough to obtain the services of a council housekeeper. Sometimes however she found that people who knew nothing about paraplegia were unable to understand why a healthy-looking young woman should have to stay in bed just because of a skin-break on her sit-upon. At such times she would have to board the children out with the Grey Sisters, warmhearted Roman Catholic nuns who conducted a Mother and Child Care Centre, or she would have to find some similar institution, until she was mobile again. Confined to bed she made what arrangements she could for herself, but she found it a depressing business. Relatives and friends were always willing to help, but both she and John dearly cherished their independence, as everyone well knew. At such times she felt very keenly the injustice of the ruling that disabled wives whose husbands earned over £13 ($26) weekly were not eligible for a pension. It would mean

170

so much to many disabled women to be able to pay for a little household help, especially at those times when they were completely out of action.

Margaret's experience as a wife and mother had given her ample opportunity to put into practice her view that it was a person's *attitude* towards his disability which decided whether or not his rehabilitation would be successful. Her own acceptance of the inevitable, her refusal to be daunted by the most formidable obstacles, her unselfconscious good humour in the face of difficulties, all these had been the result of her family background. She was never consciously 'brave' or 'heroic'. She simply got on with the business of living, and caring for those she loved, with the zest that was also characteristic of her parents. But being by nature both observant and intelligent, she could see quite clearly that many disabled people lived lives of unnecessary frustration merely because of thoughtlessness on the part of the general community. A new enlightened attitude was necessary, especially with regard to the disabled housewife and architectural barriers in general. She wished she could share her views with the general public.

The opportunity came unexpectedly. The Australian Council for Rehabilitation of Disabled was planning a rehabilitation conference. It was to be on a national basis. It was to last a full week and would be held in Melbourne in March 1965. Margaret Lester was asked to be one of the guest speakers. Her chosen subject was 'The Practical Aspects of Being a Handicapped Wife and Mother'.

The national conference had been organized by the Victorian Society for Crippled Children and Adults and the Yooralla Hospital School for Crippled Children, together with many associate members. When Margaret read the long list of distinguished medical people, therapists, social workers and others who would be taking part, her heart began to sink at the thought of addressing these experts *en masse* from a public platform, something she had never in her life done before. It was no help when John read her paper and shook his head over it.

'You can't get up there in front of all those distinguished people and describe how you bath the baby and do the family wash,' he said.

'But that's a subject on which I *am* qualified to speak,' she argued heatedly.

171

Deeply hurt, she went off to finish the new coat-dress she was making for the occasion. Her confidence was badly shaken, but she was too proud to show it.

The Saturday before the conference opened, the whole family made a rush visit to the city to buy accessories for her dress.

'You want to be proud of me when you see me sitting up there on the platform,' she said when John had chased after Karen half a dozen times and they'd spent their last penny on shoes, stockings and a new handbag. There was usually trouble getting pretty lace-ups in her size, and she could not risk any other kind for this occasion. When she was nervous her feet sometimes went into spasm, and could easily jerk a court shoe off into the middle of the audience.

'Unfortunately I won't be seeing you on the platform,' answered John. 'I'm so busy at work, and anyway that's an impossible time for me to get away. I'm sorry.'

Margaret was so disappointed that she made no reply. Glancing at her face, John thought he had better change the subject. He began to talk about Ian's engagement, which was to be announced on Easter Saturday. Doubtless there would be some kind of family celebration.

But that Easter of 1965 was to be very different from the one they had anticipated. Chocolate eggs had already been hidden in the Lester cupboards, and the notice of Ian's engagement to Carolyn had been lodged for publication, when the long-dreaded blow fell.

Gerta began to fail.

She had cheated death several times already; perhaps again her wonderful spirit and powers of recuperation would pull her through. Hoping against hope, the family gathered around her.

'We can only love her,' Margaret told herself on each unbearable visit to 'Blue Sky'. There was little else they could do.

Early on Easter Saturday she slipped quietly away.

A few months later, on 30th July, she was followed by little Phil, who for a year had been struggling bravely with an incurable illness. He was six years old.

So many years apart in age, they yet had much in common, for both were markedly endowed with an insatiable zest for life and a boundless, generous love which they bestowed on each person they met.

172

A gift so freely given can perhaps never be lost even though the giver has gone. Margaret tried to take comfort in that thought when in August her son Kim was born, a beautiful and perfect child whom she could no longer share with Gerta.

sixteen | REHABILITATION CONFERENCE: THE SUMMING UP

Natalie had come with her own two children to look after Cindy and Karen. They all came outside to say goodbye. Margaret had to avoid the clutches of forty sticky little fingers as she slid into the car and set off for the conference, which was to be held in the Ormond Hall, near Wesley College in the Melbourne suburb of Prahran.

It was good to see a familiar figure, Mrs Cheshire, rushing into the main entrance, but her heart sank lower and lower as a cheerful conference member drove her car away to park it, while someone else whizzed her chair around to the back of the hall. Here a newspaper reporter and a photographer were waiting. She answered their questions in a dream, wishing that John were with her for moral support.

The interview over, she was welcomed by the chairman of the conference, Sir John Allison.

'We're going on the platform now, my dear,' he said kindly. 'Professor Collins and Dr Oldmeadow are speaking first; then you.'

Sitting on the platform through one learned paper on The Handicapped and Parental Counselling and another on the Psycho-

174

logical Aspects of Marriage and Family Relationship, Margaret clutched her notes with shaking hands and tried to ignore the sea of faces before her. It was a help to recognize now and then someone she knew. There was Dr Cheshire, cheerfully grinning up at her, Mr Cyril Thomas, known as Cyril C., President of the Paraplegic Association, and another representative, Pamela McCarthy, whose happy face smiled from her wheelchair in the front row.

'Only a few more minutes,' she thought in a kind of panic. Sir John leaned over and whispered, 'Mrs Lester, are you sure these dates are correct? The accident, your marriage, the births of your two children?'

Margaret checked the dates in his notebook. 'Yes, they are correct.'

'Remarkable!' He rose to introduce her, and read out the dates, drawing the attention of the audience to the unusual speed of her rehabilitation. Warm applause followed his remarks. Then followed a silence. Margaret wheeled herself forward, her heart thudding so loudly that it made her feel quite ill. She opened her mouth to speak, and it seemed just then as if no words would come. At that moment a slight disturbance in the audience caught her attention. A tall young man with wildly untidy black hair was trying to creep into the hall without being noticed. He slid into a seat and wedged his briefcase between his knees. He looked up at the girl in the wheelchair on the platform, and then glanced briefly around at the audience. As clearly as if he had spoken, he seemed to be saying proudly, 'That's my wife. Isn't she wonderful?'

A great wave of love and happiness surged through Margaret, bearing away all her nervousness. Confidently she began her address.

'The motto in our house is "Anything can be done". This is the basis for our family life. I have accepted the disability of paraplegia as such, but resolved to surmount it on absolutely all occasions. Once this positive decision has been made, the major portion of rehabilitation is achieved. The remainder represents the careful planning and execution of ways and means to adapt yourself to any task. This paper will demonstrate the practical aspects of being a wife and mother. Because I must use my own experiences, it is to a certain extent a personal story, and one very much geared

175

to people in wheelchairs. The paper will be divided into four major sections—namely, the care of a family, household management, the design for living, and activities outside the home.

'First I must give a few personal historical facts. I became a paraplegic as the result of a car accident in February 1960. For me, due to a relatively high spinal fracture, this means paralysis below chest level. My legs are immobile, and there is no muscular control of the natural functions of the body. From the fracture level down, there is no power to feel hot, cold, or pain. Needless to say, balancing is also a little more difficult. Through rehabilitation, I have relearnt the activities of daily living, and now I can achieve everything in a wheelchair.

'*The care of a family.* The most significant event in my life since I became a paraplegic was my marriage, which took place nine months after the accident. My husband is a great source of inspiration to me. We share the same attitude that the wheelchair is no bar to a normal active married life. In fact, our family life is very happy and rewarding. We now have two children, aged three and a half years and twenty-one months. These children were born by caesarian section, the recommended method for paraplegic women. Although everything progressed well in both pregnancies, it was necessary to spend a month in bed before each birth. This results from the added difficulty of getting in and out of the chair, as well as the usual problem of all expectant mothers, of sitting for long periods. A third baby is due in August. At this stage I must arrange for household help for at least one month before the birth and after the return home from hospital.

'Management of babies is quite easy from a wheelchair. For instance, the baby's bath is placed on my shower seat which straddles the bath, and it is filled by a hose attached to the taps. I use the Milton method of sterilization with respect to feeding bottles, to avoid the lifting of heavy saucepans of boiling water. Lifting a baby in and out of a bassinet could present problems, but I have found that a low-sided crib is the answer. A tray is fitted at the base for storage of clothes and toilet requisites. It has castors for easy movement around the house. A napkin delivery service is essential, and I find it a handy asset to have a rotary dryer, to manage the usual piles of damp clothing which accumulate during winter.

'As babies, both children learnt to stand up at an early age, so

176

David John

Throwing the javelin

Ready for the Third Australian Paraplegic Games, 1964. Margaret with
Angus Downie of Hobart, on arrival at Adelaide Airport

that I could pick them up off the floor. At crawling and toddler stage, they also learnt to move quickly when mother called "Beep, beep" from the wheelchair. Now they command me to "beep, beep" when I bar the way to a tricycle or doll's pram.

'My two children just accept the fact that their mother is in a wheelchair. It seems natural to them, whereas other children think that if you have legs, surely you should be able to walk. The eldest daughter even imagines that one day she will be a "mummy in a chair". Children whose mothers are disabled learn to wash and dress themselves, go shopping, and take telephone messages at a very early age. My three-and-a-half-year-old enjoys washing up. She helps make the beds, and generally assists with fetching and putting things away.

'I have to ensure reasonable obedience by frequent reprimand, for safety's sake, and to save me the wasted effort of chasing the children when they are needed. There is no front fence. The girls frequently collect the mail, the milk and the paper. If they go out on to the footpath, I call—never once have they been on to the road. We also have a large fenced backyard. I never have to venture past the back verandah to fetch the children; they come when called. I have yet to determine whether these techniques would operate with young boys.

'*Household Management.* In running the home, planning ahead is most important for conserving energy. You have to teach yourself to plan and think ahead by not asking people to fetch things, even when you are wretchedly tired, or frantically doing six things at once in the kitchen.

'There is a permanent list for groceries and odds and ends— every time we run out of a commodity it is entered on the list. We shop once weekly on Saturday morning at the local supermarket, and during the week orders are phoned to the butcher and green-grocer. Most of our clothing, presents and haberdashery are ordered by telephone, as trips to town are not easy with a wheelchair and two small children. About once every three months we make an expedition to the city or large suburban shopping centre to buy shoes, material, and other articles which cannot be purchased without seeing them. In this way, unnecessary and time-consuming outings are avoided.

'You can conserve energy in household chores by wheeling from one end of the house to the other, picking up and putting away

177

in each room as you proceed. Soiled clothes are placed on the tray under the chair, so that the last port of call is the laundry.

'Again, I collect large piles of clean clothes before putting them away in appropriate places.

'Continual wheeling back and forth is tiring. Sometimes I feel like placing a notice at the front door: "No salesmen or collectors". These men frequently call at inconvenient times. One way to overcome this would be a two-way radio system between the front door and the chair.

'You can conserve energy in the kitchen by sitting in front of the open refrigerator before each meal and taking out everything that may be needed. This process is reversed after a meal. A long table at lap height is useful for the preparation and serving of meals. I frequently cook food in the electric frypan, which rests on this table. I wash up in a side-on position. Soon the sink will be lowered and the cupboards removed from underneath, so that I can wheel in frontways for better access to taps and sink bowl. A bench between the stove and sink will enable me to slide heavy saucepans, instead of lifting them over my knees.

'With the help of an automatic washing-machine and dryer, I can keep pace with the washing. A ramp and platform lead to the clothesline, and the troughs have been lowered to a suitable height.

'Let me stress that in a wheelchair you can handle all household duties, but there is a time limit. You simply take much longer to care for yourself and the family, and it requires more physical energy. Therefore outside help is required to look after the general cleaning; in my case two or three hours per week is all we can afford. I believe that a disabled wife and mother could run her house more efficiently with some regular economic assistance for household help. A permanently chairborne wife is denied the right to an invalid pension if her husband earns thirteen pounds [$26] per week or more. This eliminates most young couples with children. Yet blind people have the right to a pension regardless of any means test. One wonders why there is such a distinction between disabilities.

'Wheelchair wives are also denied the Sales Tax rebate on a new car, and on tyres. This is only allowed if the car is needed for getting to your place of employment. As we cannot walk, let alone use public transport, a car fitted with hand controls is a necessity for such things as trips to the supermarket, banks, hairdresser, and the post office. Again, the adequate care of children means trips to the health centre, doctor, dentist, and to kindergarten. Why bar the busy housewife from these benefits? After all, the housewife does an important job. Take her away—and where is the home?

'*The design for living.* Since I have so far presented to you some of the more detailed aspects of running a home, I would now like to turn to general comments about the planning required of a house.

'When first married, we shared a house, and later on moved to a terrace house in Carlton. Eighteen months afterwards we moved to a house in Balwyn. In each case most things were convenient, but ramps had to be built at the front and back doors, and where there were steps leading to bathrooms.

'With an architectural background, I have many ideas for designing a wheelchair house. To my mind the ideal plan is basically square or rectangular. Open planning of the interior eliminates doors and walls where possible, so that space is created for manoeuvring the wheelchair. Doors are at least three feet wide with a sliding mechanism. A wheel-in shower recess with a seat at a suitable height is provided in the bathroom, and ample space surrounds the toilet. A thermostatic valve which automatically regulates water temperature is desirable, and the shower rose is at a low level. A narrow kitchen seven and a half feet wide and twelve feet long is centrally placed with direct access to a covered carport. One feature of the kitchen is a sink disposal unit. The laundry, larger than is usual, serves also as a utility room. A glass wall at one end, with a view to an enclosed yard, ensures adequate supervision of young children at play.

'Other features are an abundance of storage space in low-level cupboards, and an internal incinerator to cope with the problem of rubbish disposal. Central heating is advisable when you live in a place such as Melbourne. Radiators and open fires can cause serious burning, if a paraplegic sits before them for any length of time. A disabled person's house should be relatively maintenance-free, with internal walls of exposed brickwork, timber panelling, or hardboard. Fibrous plaster is not suitable as it chips very easily when knocked with wheelchair footplates. Aluminium-framed sliding windows would be ideal.

'With all these requirements, it is not easy to buy a house "off the rack", as is now the common procedure. They tend to have timber window frames, plaster walls, and narrow passages.

It seems to me that a large building firm should be made interested in building a standard house for the disabled—one which can be included in their range of "off the rack" homes.

'*Activities outside the home*. The final section of the paper deals briefly with activities which are not directly associated with the running of a home. As a family, we have travelled many miles by car, in Victoria, New South Wales, and South Australia, camping in the car and sometimes staying at motels. Our social life is rather crowded. We visit friends, attend music concerts, and occasionally the theatre. All invitations are accepted, and we never worry about the fact that there may be stairs at our destination. People are always willing to lend a hand with the chair. On one occasion we went to a supper party in a penthouse on the fifth floor. There were ten flights of stairs and no mechanical lift.

'This is not to say that we wouldn't prefer buildings of easy access. All public buildings—that is, hospitals, churches, theatres, town halls, libraries and sports centres—should have special design features so as to be accessible to the handicapped. In this regard the American Standards Association has laid down a set of rules which need to be observed in designing public buildings. It is good to see that Melbourne's Cultural Centre will be directly accessible from the street level, and physically handicapped persons will be able to reach all galleries by means of elevators. I am also led to believe that there will be toilet compartments wide and long enough for wheelchair use.

'It would be well worth while to generally stir up the interest of architects in Australia, so that they consider disabled people when new public buildings are designed.

'A wife and mother needs the stimulus of activities which are not directly associated with the family. Disabled people can derive great pleasure from sport. My chief sport is swimming. I regularly attend an indoor heated pool. Backstroke, breaststroke and free-style provide excellent exercise for muscles which are not normally used when sitting in a chair. To my mind, the greatest disadvantage about swimming is that you have to be lifted in and out of the water. No pools in Melbourne have hydraulic hoists for this purpose, such as I have seen in America. I am pleased to comment that certain progress is being made in this direction now, as a certain engineering firm in Melbourne is currently designing a built-in hoist. If successful it will be installed in two local private pools.

'I find that dressmaking is an enjoyable pastime. An electric machine is easily used by operating the foot pedal with the right hand. Time spent in making your own clothes is worth while, as bought clothes generally need modification for the chair-bound.

'From experience I can recommend study as a stimulating activity. My architecture degree was completed after marriage. This and other activities discussed help counterbalance monotonous household chores.

'In conclusion, I reiterate that with a physical handicap, you can successfully carry out the tasks of a wife and mother. If you have the right mental approach, and if you plan your activities, you can live up to the motto, "Anything can be done".'

She was conscious of delighted and prolonged applause, she answered the interested questions, at afternoon tea she thanked dozens of people for their congratulations. But nothing seemed real until John, planting a hasty kiss on her cheek, breathed in her ear, 'It was great! You were wonderful!' before he rushed back to work. Now, she thought, she could relax. It was all over.

Actually, had she but known it, it was only just beginning, for as a result of the conference representative committees on architectural barriers were formed in various States, and Margaret was specifically invited to be a member of the Victorian committee. She accepted the nomination.

Taking the title of Architectural Standards and Design Committee of the Australian Council for Rehabilitation of Disabled, the various groups set to work. The New South Wales committee decided to follow the example of America and Britain in making their first aim the establishment of a set of standards. As a result of their efforts, on 1st February 1967 the Standards Association of Australia issued a *Draft Australian Standard Code of Recommended Practice for Building Design Requirements for the Disabled*. This was intended 'to be ancillary to the campaign to remove architectural barriers and improve the design of buildings to make them more accessible to handicapped people, who thereby obtain wider employment opportunities and are afforded greater participation as citizens'. Handicapped people were referred to as

181

those 'having disabilities interfering with normal locomotion, manual ability and co-ordination, and with disabilities of sight, hearing and age'. The Australian Council for Rehabilitation of Disabled also stressed in the preface to the draft that 'provision be made . . . for handicapped children in the design of schools in order to permit their maximum possible attendance . . . in normal schools and to avoid their segregation in special schools'. The draft will be reviewed in the light of comment received and then issued as an Australian standard.

The Victorian committee, under the chairmanship of Dr Donald Guthrie, decided first to ascertain the extent of the problem. They wanted to find out in fact how many handicapped people there were in Victoria, and what difficulties they encountered in relation to buildings and facilities, especially where employment was concerned. As a beginning they gave their support to a project which was beginning to take shape in Oakleigh, one of Melbourne's outer suburbs. The Oakleigh city council was anxious to provide what facilities and assistance it could for its aged citizens, and for this purpose a survey was being organized by Mr Oscar Roberts of the Department of Anthropology and Sociology at Monash University, the new university situated at Oakleigh. Dr Guthrie's committee, in supporting the project, suggested that the survey should also include people with general physical handicaps. The committee was also planning the construction of a standard house which should demonstrate to architects, builders, doctors and the general public the requirements necessary to enable a badly disabled person to use it.

Margaret was delighted to take part in all these schemes, especially as the Oakleigh project was to include the architectural survey of certain public buildings and transport facilities, which were her special interest.

'Why should the general public go wherever they like while *we* can't?' she exclaimed indignantly one day. 'It's thoughtless discrimination, that's what it is. It's—it's—well, it's exactly like a colour bar!'

She was particularly incensed on that occasion because she had been attending a national conference on 'Women at Work'. It had been held at one of Melbourne's biggest and most luxurious hotels, where, Margaret discovered, none of the doors to the toilets was wide enough to admit a wheelchair. In the construction of this, as of many other public buildings, only the able-bodied had been considered.

Margaret's jaunty motto 'Anything can be done' did not mean that she expected miracles to happen if only she would try hard enough. She had a perfectly clear idea of her limitations. It was within these limitations that she would never admit defeat. Not even at those times when she fell out of her wheelchair and had to lie helpless until someone else's strength came to her rescue. 'Anything can be done,' she quoted to herself ironically the next time it happened. 'That means, so far, anything except getting myself from floor level back into that wheelchair, one foot seven inches up in the air! But I'll do it some day. I *will*.'

She had been all ready to serve the breakfast while John was still fast asleep in bed. Tugging at the sheet to rouse him, she had overbalanced on to the floor.

'I've fallen out of my chair,' she said loudly, propping herself on one elbow.

'Too bad. You'll just have to stay there,' was the sleepy response as John pulled the blankets over his head, after taking a quick look to make sure she had not hurt herself.

The two little girls rushed in and began to wail loudly. 'Mummy's fallen down. Now we won't be able to have our breakfast.'

An idea flashed through Margaret's mind. 'If you want some breakfast you'll have to help Mummy first,' she said. She told them to fetch cushions—a small one and a larger one—a pillow, and the stool from the bathroom.

John opened an astonished eye.

'I read it in that book about Dr Mary Verghese, the Indian paraplegic. She fell on to the floor in her room, when studying in New York, and couldn't get back into her wheelchair. In the end she did it by raising the level she was on, a few inches at a time. If she can do it, so can I.' Margaret dragged herself about on the floor, placing the cushions, pillows and stool in a carefully graded row next to the wheelchair. With a series of strenuous push-ups, she then jerked herself from one level to the next until at last she flopped into the familiar confines of the chair.

'Well, that proves it—anything *can* be done,' she thought with satisfaction. 'It's just a matter of thinking out a new method.'

There was no fanfare of trumpets when, almost a hundred and

fifty years ago, a great musician who was deaf started to compose a choral symphony based on the poet Schiller's 'Ode to Joy'. Nor when, nearly eighty years ago, a blind, deaf and dumb little girl suddenly realized that the fingers of a friend were tapping out a pattern that meant water.

All that happened in the Lester house that morning was that John went back to sleep and the little girls trotted happily off to the kitchen, pleased that their mother would give them their breakfast as usual.

So often in life the moments of greatest significance pass unnoticed and are only recognized in retrospect. Perhaps it is just as well.

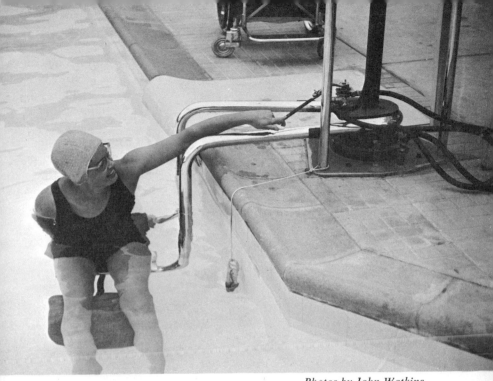

Above: the pool at 'Blue Sky'; entering the water alone by means of the hydraulic hoist. *Below*: the Lester family at home, 1966. John, Kim, Margaret, Karen, Cindy

Photos by
John Watkins

Margaret the mermaid,
March 1967

EPILOGUE

Grandad Watkins had gone rapidly downhill over the past few years. His wife, Nonnie Watkins, had died soon after the birth of Margaret's second daughter. Unable to look after himself, he was installed in a flat specially built on to 'Blue Sky', until he needed more skilled nursing. Knowing that he was nearing the end, he asked from his hospital bed for his son to suggest a way in which his savings could be used for the benefit of all the family, particularly Margaret.

John and Gerta had often daydreamed about building a swimming pool designed and equipped so that Margaret and her paraplegic friends could enjoy swimming without the usual problems of being helped in and out of the water. It was to be a place where they could come whenever they wanted to exercise their disabled bodies, and enjoy the freedom of movement usually denied them. And they must be able to do all this without the need of any outside assistance whatsoever.

When John described this idea to Grandad, the old man begged him to find out the cost and discuss it with his bank manager. On being told that it could be done with the money available, the frail old body relaxed and Grandad's face eased into a beaming smile. 'That's it then, John. Promise me you'll carry it through and I'm happy.'

Excitement over the project brought Gerta much joy, too, although at that time her own strength was rapidly failing. She sat contentedly in the car while John sought for ideas, inspected equipment and discussed details with pool builders. But neither she nor Grandad were to see the project completed, for he died only a few weeks after she did.

By this time the first steps towards the construction of the pool had already been taken. John continued with it according to his father's wishes. Working out the details absorbed most of his spare time and helped to distract him during those sorrowful and difficult months.

The pool was to be built on the side lawn immediately below 'Blue Sky'. It was to be safely fenced, with locking gates, but easy of access for wheelchairs. It must be within reach of a toilet; there would be a little changing room; the water would be heated. Margaret could use it whenever she wished, even if there were no one at the house, because the main feature, the pool's pride and glory, was to be a hydraulic-powered hoist. This was a seat on which paralysed people could raise or lower themselves into the water completely under their own control. The one her father was designing to be built by a Melbourne engineering firm would be completely self-operable. So far as they knew, it would be the first of its kind in Melbourne.

'It will be finished in time for Phillip's twenty-first birthday,' her father promised her. 'So we can christen it that night: the Arthur A. Watkins Memorial Swimming Pool.'

He knew that it would be a difficult occasion for them all without Gerta, especially as Phillip had planned to announce his engagement at the same time; he decided that a small theatre party followed by supper and a swim in the new pool would be an appropriate way of celebrating the occasion.

It was mostly a family party, with a few close friends. 'Blue Sky', when they eventually reached it, was brightly lit, the tables generously loaded with delicacies such as Gerta had always loved to provide. In the garden the silvery-blue water of the pool reflected the coloured lights John had put up in Phillip's honour. It made a picturesque setting, in which Phillip and Denise wandered about as happy as a pair of school-children. Phillip had graduated

186

from Dookie Agricultural College earlier in the year. He had all sorts of plans for the future, and they did not include a long engagement. Ian, now training to be a pilot for Qantas, had flown from Sydney, glad of the opportunity to be with Carolyn for the evening. Natalie and her husband Cliff, Margaret and John were all revelling in the evening's freedom from their lively young families. Fifteen-year-old Josephine, helped by various friends and relatives, looked after the guests as unselfconsciously as her mother would have done. It was a quiet party; at times there was a kind of listening atmosphere, as though people were waiting for the voice and presence of someone who had not yet appeared.

Soon after midnight John Watkins led little Phil's parents, June and Julius, through the garden to the swimming pool. It was a mild, still night late in November. Although summer was so close the air still held the freshness of spring, and the fragrance of spring flowers mingled with the unmistakable scent of the Australian bush—for John and Gerta had put many native trees and plants in their garden. From the house came the faint echoes of young voices. Under the stars the distant ranges were darkly outlined; all light seemed to be centred on the pool, where one or two people were already frolicking. They stood watching.

'Gerta would have revelled in this,' said June, expressing the thought of them all.

'She would indeed,' replied John quietly. 'Aren't you two swimming?'

'No thank you, John. I think we should go home, but we're waiting to see Margaret in the pool. We've never seen her swim since the accident.'

Presently Margaret came towards them, smiling, in her wheelchair, with John Lester walking beside her. He and John Watkins were anxious that she should know exactly how to work the hydraulic seat-lift. Once she had done it correctly they would leave her to cope on her own. Her father showed her how the seat swung out over the water, and then lowered itself gently to the required depth. He brought it back to the exact level of her wheelchair and swung it around beside her. John Lester watched carefully on this first occasion to make sure that the wheelchair would not slip on the edge of the pool.

'I think I've got it,' said Margaret. 'Let me try now.' She slid across on to the flat seat, pulled the lever, swung herself out over the water, and the seat descended slowly. She floated off it gently and lay on her back looking up at them with an expression of incredulous delight.

'But it's absolutely wonderful!' she exclaimed joyfully. 'It's a hundred times better even than I'd imagined it!'

She turned, and with the grace and agility of a mermaid, went skimming through the water to the other side of the pool.

The four who watched were deeply moved. So much had happened to them all in time past; so many mutual experiences of joy or pain had led to their being together, this night, to share yet another.

'I can see now why you built the pool,' said June. 'It was worth it just for this moment.'

John Watkins nodded. 'Yes, it was.'

Walking back to the car, she felt her husband squeeze her hand. 'Yes, I know,' she said. They often read each other's thoughts. 'You are going to say that when God closes one door He opens another.'

'No, as a matter of fact I was trying to remember the words of that Indian poem we found.'

She said slowly, out of the darkness:

> 'Even the severed branch grows again,
> And the sunken moon returns:
> Wise men who ponder this
> Are not troubled in adversity.'

APPENDIX

WHAT IS PARAPLEGIA?

by D. J. E. Cheshire, Director, Spinal Injuries Centre, Austin Hospital, Heidelberg, Victoria.

Paraplegia is the medical name for a condition which results from injury or disease of the spinal cord—the main nerve trunk running down from the brain, within the bony spinal column. When the spinal cord is injured no messages are able to pass from the brain to the muscles to cause movement, nor can messages of sensation be carried from the extremities to the brain. The result is that there is complete paralysis below the level at which the injury has occurred, and the person is unable to move or feel part of his trunk and his legs. There is often paralysis of the functions of the bladder, bowel and sexual organs as well.

In some cases the injury is higher and involves the neck part of the spine. In this case the paralysis is much more extensive and involves the whole trunk, and part, or all, of the arms. It is then termed quadriplegia and a person with this type of spinal-cord injury is known as a quadriplegic.

Paraplegia may be caused by injury, illness or a congenital defect. In the injury group, by far and away the commonest cause

191

in Australia is the motor car accident: this single cause accounts for fifty-five per cent of all paraplegias due to injury which occur in the State of Victoria. Other causes are industrial accidents, sporting accidents—especially diving into shallow water—and falls in and around the home. Paraplegia may also be caused by illness: sometimes it occurs in young people and sometimes in older people, in whom it may be an incident in a long-standing and progressive condition.

Of those paraplegics who have had accidents, about ninety per cent are men, and the great majority of them are young men between the ages of sixteen and thirty years. They are fit young men who, because of an accident, have lost the ability to walk. They are not sick, and they are not invalids—they are fit young men who cannot walk. In fact, one may say that in order to live successfully as a paraplegic, one must be as fit as a top-class athlete above the waist, even though one is paralysed below the waist. These are people who have a whole life ahead of them, and for whom no efforts expended in total rehabilitation can be too great.

CHRONOLOGY SHOWING MILESTONES IN MARGARET LESTER'S REHABILITATION

1st February 1960
Accident at Mullengandra. Admission to Albury and District General Hospital with crushed chest, broken ribs, bruising of left lung, haemorrhage into chest cavity, severe concussion, fractured jaw, bruises and lacerations, bad shock, severe fracture-dislocation of the upper part of the thoracic spine with damage to the spinal cord resulting in paralysis below chest level.

3rd February 1960
Admission to the Acute Ward of Spinal Injuries Centre, Austin Hospital, Heidelberg.

8th April 1960
First time in wheelchair.

29th April 1960
Transfer to Rehabilitation Ward 17 and commencement of rigorous training programme in gymnasium.

31st August 1960
Discharge from hospital to take job at the Ideal Homes Exhibition demonstrating an exhibit to members of the public.

19th November 1960
Marriage to John Lester.

5th August 1961
Birth of her first child.

193

CONVERSION OF AN AVERAGE SUBURBAN HOUSE INTO ONE SUITABLE FOR A WHEELCHAIR HOUSEWIFE

(The Lesters did this gradually over a period of four years as money became available)

1. A small wooden ramp was built from the front door over the step into the garden.
2. The door between toilet and laundry was removed to allow access.
3. The bathroom door was removed to allow access.
4. A wooden bath-seat was made to fit across the bath. It had a back for support and a piece of wood underneath at each side to prevent it from slipping. An ordinary plastic shampoo hose was then slipped on to the hot and cold water taps and secured with elastic, to make an easily controlled shower.
5. The back verandah had a false wooden floor put over it to make it the same level as the rest of the house.
6. A wooden ramp was put from the verandah into the garden near the rotary clothes-line. A balustrade was added for safety.
7. The kitchen sink was lowered to suitable wheelchair height. The underneath cupboard was removed so that the sink could be approached from the front. The waterpipes underneath were well lagged to prevent the legs from being knocked or burnt.
8. The floor level of the kitchen cupboards was raised to a height of nine inches from the floor so that the footplates of the chair could go into the resulting space when a paraplegic was working at the kitchen bench. This was to prevent damage to the cupboards by the footplates, or damage to feet by accidental bumping.

194

SELECTED BIBLIOGRAPHY

General books on disability:

Ayrault, Evelyn West, *Take One Step* (Methuen, London 1965).
Brown, Christy, *My Left Foot* (Secker and Warburg, London 1954).
Fraser, Ian (ed.), *Conquest of Disability* (Odhams Press, London 1956).
Killilea, Marie, *Karen* (World's Work, Surrey 1953).
Lawrence, Marjorie, *Interrupted Melody* (Invincible Press, Sydney 1949).
Marshall, Alan, *I Can Jump Puddles* (F. W. Cheshire, Melbourne 1955); *This is the Grass* (F. W. Cheshire 1962).
Opie, June, *Over My Dead Body* (Methuen, London 1957; Pan Books, London 1958).
Roesler, J. H., *God's Second Door* (Rehandar, Hamilton, Victoria).
Russell, Wilfred, *New Lives for Old*, The Story of the Cheshire Homes (Gollancz, London 1963).
Viscardi, Henry jnr, *Give Us the Tools* (World's Work, Surrey 1959).
Wilson, Dorothy Clarke, *Take My Hands*, The Remarkable Story of Dr Mary Verghese of Vellore (Hodder and Stoughton, London 1964).

Journals:

Australian Paraplegic (official organ of the Australian Paraplegic Council, published quarterly by the Paraplegic Association of W.A.).

Cord, The, International Journal for Paraplegics (published quarterly by Stoke Mandeville National Spinal Injuries Centre, Aylesbury).

Easter Seal Bulletin (published monthly by the National Society for Crippled Children and Adults, Inc. Chicago, Illinois), vol. 24, No. 8.

Fortitude (official magazine of the Civilian Maimed and Limbless Association of New South Wales, published quarterly).

Honga (magazine of the Old Camberwell Grammarians' Association), August 1963, 'Vale Ken Slater'.

Paravics Monthly Newsletter (official organ of the Paraplegic Association of Victoria).

Patchwork (official school magazine of the Presbyterian Ladies' College, Melbourne), 75th annual number; No. 91 new series, December 1950; No. 93 new series, December 1952.

Rehabilitation in Australia (published quarterly by the Australian Council for Rehabilitation of Disabled).

Other official publications:

Australian Council for Rehabilitation of Disabled, *National Rehabilitation Conference* (Melbourne, 29th March-2nd April 1965).

British Standards Institution Council for Codes of Practice, *Draft of British Standard Code of Practice for Access to Buildings for the Disabled* (issued October 1965, and shortly to be published).

Caniff, Charles E., Executive Director of Association of Rehabilitation Centres, U.S.A., *Architectural Barriers—A Personal Problem.*

Chatelain, Leon jnr, Past President American Institute of Architects, Washington, D.C., *Architectural Barriers—A Blueprint for Action.*

Goldsmith, Selwyn, *Designing for the Disabled* A Manual of Technical Information (Technical Information Service, Royal Institute of British Architects).

Haverstock, Henry W. jnr, Chairman, Architectural Barriers Committee, Minnesota Society for Crippled Children and Adults, *Minnesota Story.*

Institute of Physical Medicine and Rehabilitation, New York University Medical Centre, *Primer for Paraplegics and Quadriplegics* (1960).

International Stoke Mandeville Games for the Paralysed in Tokyo, 1964 (general report published by the International Committee of the Stoke Mandeville Games 1964, Great Britain).

Laase, Leroy T., Ph.D., Chairman and Professor of Speech, University of Nebraska, *Organising for Community Action.*

196

Nugent, Timothy, Assistant Professor and Director, Student Rehabilitation Center, University of Illinois, *Design of Buildings to Permit their Use by the Physically Handicapped* A National attack on architectural barriers (co-sponsored by the National Society for Crippled Children and Adults and the President's Committee on Employment of the Physically Handicapped. Reprinted from *New Building Research*, Fall 1960. Publication 910, Building Research Institute).

President's Committee on Employment of the Physically Handicapped and the National Society for Crippled Children and Adults, U.S.A., *Architectural Barriers and the Handicapped.*

Saltman, Jules, *Paraplegia: A Head, a Heart and Two Big Wheels* (Public Affairs Pamphlet No. 300, U.S.A.).

Spastic Children's Society of Victoria, *Sixteenth Annual Report.*

Standards Association of Australia, *Draft Australian Standard Code of Recommended Practice for Building Design Requirements for the Disabled* (1967).

Trebilcock, Arthur F., Chairman, Governor's Committee on Employment of the Physically Handicapped, Madison, Wisconsin, *Legislation in Wisconsin.*

Victorian Society for Crippled Children and Adults, *Thirteenth Annual Report.*

Walsh, J. J., M.D., Deputy Director, National Spinal Injuries Centre, Stoke Mandeville Hospital, Aylesbury, Bucks, *Understanding Paraplegia* (Tavistock Publications, London 1964).